WHY DEMOCRACY FAILED

And Ideas for Something Better

Contents

Introduction

Back in the days when monarchs were fashionable, no one imagined there could be a better approach to governance. The monarch, anointed by Divine Will, would be wise and just. And if the monarch was in fact a hopeless incompetent, well, that was just God's Will working in a mysterious way. As usual.

With the benefit of hindsight we can see that the institution of monarchy was nothing more than tribal leadership writ large. As a primate group species we humans evolved within small groups in which following the leader was paramount and essential for the group's survival. Being relatively weak, slow, and vulnerable we humans can survive only as part of a group. After the agricultural revolution and the development of permanent settlements these groups expanded to become tribes and eventually to become nations. Yet regardless of size, we retained the core concept of hierarchy with the leader firmly on top. It's natural for us to play follow-the-leader, even when the leader is frankly a bit of a disappointment. Today, when most Western citizens live in quite different circumstances, we still understand instinctively what it meant for Agamemnon to be a King.

As societies grew in complexity and as technological developments during the Renaissance and thereafter began to erode the myth-based power of the priesthood, the divine right of monarchs to rule slowly waned. Seeking to minimize the harm an incompetent ruler could inflict and also seeking greater stability and regularity of law, first assemblies of barons and then later formal Parliaments began to agitate for greater powers and responsibilities. The demands of Parliaments and similar such assemblies were difficult to reject when the monarch's finances so often were in a parlous state due to some unnecessary war or a hopelessly inept approach to taxation. And thus, very slowly, the power of monarchs ebbed away and the power of Parliaments increased.

As Parliaments increasingly took over the job of legislating and taxing it became necessary to acquire some degree of legitimacy and to balance the various competing interests always inherent in a large nation comprising many different types of class and occupation. As nations were too large to permit an Athenian model whereby all eligible citizens could assemble on a regular basis to take decisions, the notion of representatives arose. The concept was simple: a town or borough would elect a representative who would carry its interests to the Parliament.

Unfortunately for the concept of representation, however, reality turned out to be rather different. Hundreds of individual representatives milling around in a Parliament could never effect any meaningful action. Imagine a dinner party in which three hundred people are all talking at the same time and no one is listening to anyone else. What quickly happened was that representatives realized they needed to group together on the basis of shared interests in order to be effective. And thus the first political Parties were born. What few historians and even fewer members of the ordinary public seem to have realized is that this was a fundamental change to the notion of representative democracy.

When individuals cluster together to form a Party, it's inevitable that a great many interests must be abandoned in favor of a smaller number of interests that the group collectively can agree on. Initially these interests were predicated by class: landowners clubbed together to promote policies that favored landowners; later groups representing tradespeople and the "middle classes" emerged; later still organized labor found political voice through Parties dedicated to representing the interests of the proletariat. But as society grew more complex and interests expanded beyond simple class lines, political Parties found they had to appeal to a wider range of constituents whose interests were not particularly obvious and whose opinions were increasingly shaped by the mass media. Individual politicians increasingly gravitated towards Parties that seemed likely to win elections.

And thus the supposed representatives came no longer to really represent the interests of the towns and boroughs that elected them but instead to represent at best only a modest sub-set championed by the Party to whom they belong. Meanwhile those same representatives came to enjoy the power and privileges that go along with being a formal member of a Parliament. Over time this trend grew so that political Parties increasingly looked for policies they believed would be attractive enough to secure them votes regardless of their net impact on the nation, because staying in power became the over-riding objective. Policies are thus sold to the electorate by their supposed representatives, the most successful salespeople get re-elected, and the whole process continues on its merry way, a self-perpetuating game of buy-a-vote.

In other words, far from representing the interests of the electorate, politicians became salespeople for the policies of their Party, policies designed to appeal to immediate impulses and crude desires. The phrase "representative democracy" is therefore a complete misnomer. There is no representation. Somehow we've all managed to gloss over this rather important detail.

What this means is that citizens are in effect largely disenfranchised. Mary comes knocking on our door and tells us all about the wonderful policies her Party is promising. A few minutes later Jim turns up and likewise tries to sell us his Party's shiny new policies. We may not actually agree with either Mary or Jim, but perhaps we disagree slightly less with Mary so we vote for her. Sadly, the one policy we agreed with is subsequently dropped from the Party's legislative agenda so even though we voted for Mary we end up with nothing to show for it.

This is the baleful situation in a first-past-the-post system such as seen in the United Kingdom and the United States of America, among others. In a proportional representation system the outcome is even worse, for coalitions must be built and the policies they ultimately implement will bear no relationship to anything any of the voters thought they were voting for. Yet who can be blamed? No one can predict in advance the horse-trading necessary to build and sustain a coalition government. So in proportional systems every voter is perpetually disenfranchised.

If we're honest, representative democracy doesn't seem to be living up to its hype. Yet we're assured, *pace* Churchill, that it's better than all the other systems of government that have from time to time been tried. So that's all right, then.

Except of course it's not. We've come to expect continuous improvement in nearly every aspect of our everyday lives. We'd be very unhappy if we went into a showroom to buy a new car and the only thing on offer was the Model T Ford and the salesman said, "Well, it's not a very good automobile but it is better than all the other automobiles that have from time to time been assembled" and left it at that. We'd be even less happy if all commercial air travel today relied on the Wright brothers' Flyer because it is just a little bit better than a Montgolfier balloon. And we'd doubtless be very unhappy indeed if when we needed an operation our doctor sat on a wooden chair reading Galen in Latin while a barber-surgeon (who understands no Latin at all) saws away at our leg, as used to happen not so very long ago.

Today we have cheap wrist-watches accurate to one second per year, smartphones that instantly connect us to anyone anywhere on the planet and access the world's knowledge with a few taps of a finger. We have automobiles that are incomparably more comfortable and far safer than anything on the road thirty years ago and we have aircraft that reliably whisk us around the globe in such safety that we distract ourselves by complaining about the quality of the in-flight meal. Everything around us is subject to continuous improvement to better meet our needs.

Yet our systems of government have not improved. If anything, they have become increasingly overwhelmed by the demands of a complex and inter-connected world. It is no exaggeration to say that today we're witnessing the collapse of representative democracy. Hoping that representative democracy can cope with the complexities of the modern world is akin to hoping that a mechanical Babbage calculating machine could somehow be used to underpin today's Internet or that steam engines could somehow be tinkered with so they can launch satellites into orbit.

Lest anyone claim that representative democracy is still a viable approach to government, let's take a quick look to see how well it is doing. Representative democracy is, after all, aspirational. Everyone down to the dullest-witted tyrant wants to be seen as democratic because democracy is modern and shiny and grand and who doesn't want to be modern and shiny and grand? We're all democracies now! But what does that actually mean, when we strip away the veneer of Political Correctness?

Across most of Africa representative democracy is a violent sham in which the leader of the largest tribe suppresses members of the smaller tribes in order to loot as much of the nation's wealth as possible and eventually install his son or wife as his successor so the looting can remain a wholesome family business.

Across much of South America representative democracy is a populist mess that reliably generates violence and financial defaults, along with chronic shortages of basic consumer goods.

Across much of Asia representative democracy is a thin veneer beneath which the military exercises real power or thinly conceals dictatorships in all but name.

In Russia and in the various -stans that comprised most of the former USSR, representative democracy is the term used for *de facto* dictatorship for life. As they say around the Kremlin, "One man, one vote. Putin is the one man, and his is the one vote." But Putin is a naïve latecomer compared to the tyrants of Uzbekistan, Tajikistan, Turkmenistan, and all the other fly-blown unfortunate central Asian nations the rest of the world prefers to ignore.

Which leaves us staring uncomfortably at North America and at Europe. If anyone can say with a straight face that a system which delivers Trump and Brexit is fit for purpose, there's a job waiting for them as press secretary for the People's Democratic Republic of North Korea.

So it's apparent that democracy is collapsing, overwhelmed by an unstoppable wave of populism/nationalism in which complex problems are purportedly to be solved by simple-minded non-solutions.

The First Big Question is: how could this possibly happen to a system of governance that is supposedly so much better than all the other systems that have from time to time been tried? How could nominally educated voters in developed nations, enjoying standards of living unknown in human history, rush to elect incompetent idiots whose policies are guaranteed to destroy everything we value?

And the Second Big Question is: if we accept that representative democracy has grown threadbare and understand it is about to be swept away and will be followed inevitably by an interregnum of tyranny, abuse, folly, and resultant horrors, what should our grand-children attempt to put in its place many years from now when the survivors, standing amid rubble and despair, say to themselves, "hey, let's not do that again?"

This is going to be a very unfashionable book. It's not going to claim that the problems of democracy can only be solved by more democracy. If you believe that, you must also believe the US National Rifle Association when it claims (as it always does after every mass shooting) that the violence engendered by having 400 million guns in a society of 330 million people can only be solved by (yes, you guessed it) having even more guns.

This book is going to take a look at representative democracy with open eyes and frankly we're going to find it completely unfit for purpose. We'll see how democracy limped along in the days prior to instantaneous mass communication and how it was never much good even back then. We'll look at the inevitable outcomes of any system that depends on soliciting the votes of largely uninformed and thoughtless citizens: the vote-buying, the lies, the economic distortions, and the unfair imposition of costs on everyone who can't sit down at the big table and buy a sufficient number of politicians.

Finally we'll look at potential replacements for representative democracy. Replacements that not only seek to circumvent the many weaknesses of our present systems of governance but also take into account the fact that we're a group species with a significant set of hardwired behaviors that are counter-rational yet must be accommodated if any such system is to persist over time.

Above all else this book aims to be realistic. We understand that you can't get to *there* (a more adequate approach to governance) from *here*, because most people always resist change and cling on to what they know even when it's failing them. We also understand that building castles in the air is a beguiling but utterly futile pursuit. Anything that doesn't take into account human nature with all its warts and obstructions is going to fall flat at the first hurdle. Just ask Karl Marx, a Grade A Castle-in-the-Air Builder if ever there was one. And we're not going to waste time on absurdities like the "benevolent autocrat" or an "enlightened elite."

This book is intended not only for readers who are alive today but primarily for our descendants who, having survived the coming decades of entirely unnecessary horrors, may one far-distant day be looking around for better ideas than the systems of government we today passively accept as inevitable. All we can ask is that you read this book with an open mind and then put it in a waterproof wrapping in the hope that your grand-children may be curious enough to open it up sixty years from now and potentially find something of value. After all, neither Locke nor Montesquieu could possibly have imagined there would come into existence, many years after they penned their seminal works, a group of American colonists seeking to create an entirely new and self-regulating system of government. Yet had Locke and Montesquieu and others not written, the colonists would have had little to seed their thoughts and guide their hands as they fashioned their entirely novel approach to governance.

We can only hope that this book, and many yet to be written by other authors, may have a similar beneficial influence years from now when those who have passed through the darkness to come will be looking for more adequate approaches to the problems inherent in governance.

The Child That Grew and Grew

Democracy as we know it today didn't begin as an intentional system of governance. Our present democracies grew out of very humble beginnings in an entirely unconscious way, unguided and with lots of unintended consequences along the road.

Back in the early days, life for European monarchs was a bit like an extended family sleep-over. Everyone knew everyone else, often a bit too well for comfort. The King, or more rarely the Queen, would have plenty of cousins with nearly equal claim to the throne. Many of these close relatives would be dreaming about the glorious day when they would ascend to the pinnacle and place the crown upon their own head. And so, in fact, it often turned out. Generally the only way a monarch managed to get through an entire reign without being defenestrated was by carefully managing the balance of power between himself and the "reserve bench" of barons, each of whom possessed his own private army with which to press any case he might have.

Over time the rights of the barons grew and often acted as a legal as well as a *de facto* check on the monarch's supposedly absolute power. While this wasn't much fun for the monarch it was a great deal better than being deposed and executed in some imaginatively unpleasant manner, and so by and large such arrangements became customary. And for a while, everything was more or less stable and predictable in the land.

But then things changed, as they always do. Underneath the barons, in time, there developed a caste of wealthy merchants and they too had interests they wanted to promote. And then there were the craft guilds which had their own form of power and influence. All of these various players had to be included in the game, some officially and some obliquely depending on local circumstance. Civic life became increasingly complicated and monarchs who failed sufficiently to accommodate the various powerful groups would ultimately find that their magnificence was somewhat more tenuous than they might have wished.

Slowly therefore, as democracy evolved beyond barons keeping wayward kings in line, the franchise expanded. It became clear that the enfranchised would tend to create laws that favored them at the expense of the disenfranchised and so naturally enfranchisement became highly valued. At first only men of rank could have influence, then men above a certain threshold of wealth achieved enfranchisement, and gradually the wealth criterion was weakened so that more and more people secured the vote. Although many abuses such as "rotten boroughs" survived for a very long time, the direction was clear: if democracy was good, then more democracy was better.

Unfortunately no one stopped to ask some fundamental questions about representative democracy because each step along the way was merely an expedient designed to defuse immediate tensions. No one sat down and thought about where it was all going. We take for granted what's already here, and then we tinker with things from time to time, and in general we just hope for the best. We also project our hopes and dreams onto those who have power and prestige. For a very long time, though it's difficult to believe now, a lot of people equated rank with capability. The phrase "our betters" was not uncommon in Europe even as recently as one hundred years ago. In the USA the situation was slightly different insofar as wealth was assumed to be the ultimate mark of virtue and competence. A wealthy man is therefore an important man. In other words, the USA simply created its own aristocracy from those skilled at the acquisition of large fortunes. The overall assumption that rank, however it should be defined, implied competence survived despite an endless stream of empirical evidence to the contrary.

The British, to take one nation as an example, really should have known better. For generations the British military, like the French and Germans and Polish and pretty much every other European nation, drew its officer class from the ranks of the privileged. Good chaps simply knew how to lead, it was in their blood, very possibly something to do with fox hunting and the molesting of servant girls. Which is why, to give merely one example among many, in 1842 the British Army benefited so tremendously from the leadership of Major General Sir William Elphinstone who abandoned a secure and well-provisioned fortress in Kabul in favor of leading nearly seventeen thousand people (mainly women and children) in the depths of winter through the most inhospitable territory on the planet. Astonishingly, this masterful plan did not end well. A single British military officer and a handful of Indian sepoys staggered out of the Khyber Pass many days later; everyone else either froze to death or was massacred by Afghan tribesmen who picked them off as they trudged exhausted and starving through one blizzard after another.

So much for the "good chaps" whose leadership abilities were "in their blood."

Lest we assume such blunders are only possible when dealing with a landowning aristocracy, we can note that today the USA has squatting toad-like at the top of the heap a particularly egregious and intellectually stunted buffoon whose primary attraction to his supporters is that he is rich, even though his wealth is almost entirely a product of his father's doing.

What do such examples have to do with democracy at large? Well, the notion of representative democracy rests in no small measure on the assumption that representatives will be able to discharge their responsibilities with at least a modicum of competence. For a very long time rank and wealth have been assumed to be proxies for ability. We can presume that those who died under Elphinstone's command would be unlikely to support this notion wholeheartedly, and the merest glance at Trump's catastrophically inept administration likewise undermines any argument in its favor. Today, though politicians are in general more careful about attempting to appear as "one of the people," the vast majority are still well-connected and come overwhelmingly from the top socio-economic strata. Meanwhile their leadership abilities remain scant despite all claims to the contrary.

The second and even more tenuous notion underpinning democracy is that voters will weigh up policies and the character of politicians and come to rational conclusions based on evidence and probability and then vote accordingly.

Once we've all stopped laughing and crying, the serious point is that clearly neither of these two criteria have ever been met in any instantiation of democracy anywhere on our planet. When we actually look at history what we see is a pile of incompetence, ignorance, incoherence, and idiocy that would put to shame even the most cynical satirical television comedy production.

Aha, one might shout (if one was given to shouting "aha," that is…), what about World War II? Didn't democracy triumph over dictatorship? Didn't democracy save the world from tyranny?

Well, actually, no. Democracy enabled World War II to happen in the first place. There's a wealth of documentation to show that powerful forces within Germany were ready to depose Hitler at the time he took the huge gamble of marching a small number of troops into the Rhineland. If the British or the French, the supposed "Great Powers" of the day, had lifted a finger to oppose this blatant violation of the Treaty of Versailles, Hitler would have been out of office and back in jail before you could say *Entschuldigen sie, Obergruppenführer*. What actually occurred, however, was that Chamberlain and Daladier, the leaders of Britain and France, were so timorous and so influenced by the desire of their citizens for "peace at any price" that they hid their heads under embroidered bedsheets and pretended nothing of significance had occurred.

This masterful hiding-under-the-bed strategy continued as Hitler went on to build up his military assets in contravention of the Treaty of Versailles and continued to annex territories until such time as he felt ready to wage a massive European war. In Britain and France, fearful citizens applauded the game of hide-under-the-bed because it was so much more pleasant than confronting reality and thinking about where this all would inevitably lead.

So democracy was what enabled Hitler to succeed. The British, who love to claim they "won the war" much as the French love to claim that every single French citizen (including those not yet born) was in the Resistance, forget that the reason they ended up fighting Nazi Germany was because Winston Churchill resolutely ignored "the will of the people" and insisted on standing up to German aggression despite overwhelming evidence that the British people were still rather keen on remaining under the bed, thank you very much. Given the chance of a referendum it is undoubtedly the case that a majority of British voters would have voted to capitulate to Hitler.

And as for "democracy triumphing over tyranny" we can simply note that it was the Soviet Union that drained much of Hitler's military and industrial capacity. This plus the huge materiel advantage of the USA is what actually won the war, neither of which had very much to do with democracy at all. And as for the moral superiority of democracy, immediately after the war in Europe was concluded the "great democracies" were happy to consign hundreds of millions of Europeans to what amounted to little more than slavery by ceding all of Eastern Europe to Stalin, and all too happy to turn a blind eye to Stalin's execution of tens of thousands of brave Poles, Czechs, and others who'd fought against the Nazis and were thus deemed an "impediment" to the magnificent postwar plans of the glorious Soviet Union.

The USA also became the only nation on the planet (to date) to use thermonuclear weapons to kill hundreds of thousands of unarmed civilians merely in order that President Truman could feel fractionally less intimidated by Joseph Stalin. Afterward the West was eager to embrace and embroider upon the fiction that this atrocity was necessary in order to end the war in the Pacific but all documents show clearly that the Japanese surrendered because the Soviets invaded Manchuria. In fact the Japanese High Command seems not to have paid any attention to Hiroshima and Nagasaki during its critical period of deliberations and may not even have been aware of what had happened to those two cities.

So if that's our much-vaunted "triumph of democracy" one dreads to imagine what failure would look like.

It's a cliché that history is written by the victors and so the democracies wrote histories in which they appeared as the vanquishing heroes. The stories continue today. Democracy is what makes societies stable, law-abiding, and ultimately wealthy, we're told. As the British Empire crumbled (it was all very well exploiting the colonies, but being expected to help them develop was quite another matter entirely) it became fashionable to proclaim that All Shall Be Well if only everyone became democratic. Thus a thin veneer of representative democracy was painted on top of deeply tribal societies in order to assuage Western consciences and permit tribal leaders to loot their countries in a perfectly legal and utterly democratic way. It seemed to occur to no-one that a few minor features such as rule of law, an independent judiciary, a free press, and a reasonably free market economy might in fact be essential prerequisites for democracy to stand any temporary chance whatsoever.

Liberated from the need to think about such things, the European powers decolonized and the USA elected itself Principle Cheer-Leader for democracy, eventually becoming famous for hectoring developing nations on the importance of democratically treating all citizens equally while continuing to practice enormous racial discrimination and violence at home and continuing to depose democratically-elected leaders in various developing nations abroad. Perhaps not surprisingly, many leaders of developing nations were a trifle skeptical and continued to maintain a firm grip on the reins of power, even if that did occasionally require holding a rigged election just to show everyone how thoroughly democratic they were.

Although representative democracy largely failed to take hold in any meaningful form outside of Western Europe and the Antipodes, this failure was for some time concealed by the fact of the Cold War. One cannot be overly critical of one's own system of government when it appears that any day the entire planet may be turned into a radioactive cinder. As the twentieth century wore on, however, the deficiencies of the Soviet command economy became so blatant that even the most ardent apologist could not disguise the fact that when it came to the rudimentary business of providing its people with the basics of life, the USSR was an abject failure. Soviet citizens became adept at standing in queues, hoping that several hours spent in the freezing cold might yield perhaps a half-roll of semi-adequate toilet paper or even (dare one hope?) a sausage that wasn't entirely moldy. Contrasted with the wealth and abundance of the West it was clear that the Soviet approach to life was not worthy of emulation. So people confused the relative success of a semi-free market economy with the success of representative democracy, and drew entirely the wrong conclusions.

The contest between market-oriented democracies and command-oriented tyrannies was akin to a contest between someone sticking glass into their legs and another person shooting themselves in the head. Yes, when it is all over the wounded person seems to have done better than the headless one. But that's not really the point, is it?

Democracy and its Discontents

If there is one thing we humans are excellent at, it is drawing the wrong conclusions. Back in the 1970s the USA was convinced that Japan would soon out-pace it and dominate the world economy. Today many in the USA are convinced that China will soon out-pace it and dominate the world economy. While China's economic progress has been very impressive over the last twenty-five years it nevertheless remains essentially a quasi-command economy and history shows that life is far too complex for such an approach to work over extended periods of time. Tyrants desire above all else to hold onto power; this means they must repress, control, and select. In consequence, economic vitality is slowly eroded. Rent-seeking by apparatchiks becomes the predominant focus and this in turn further limits investment and innovation. It's relatively easy for an undeveloped economy to play catch-up by copying Western innovations but much more difficult to sustain internal innovation when almost every aspect of life is determined by decisions from above.

As China moves ever further down the road of social control and repression by such means as implementing "social scores" whereby each and every individual will be assessed on a range of Party-friendly positions, it is impossible to imagine the future emergence and triumph of mavericks like Bill Gates, Larry Ellison, and Steve Jobs even on a small scale. And thus China will stifle its ability to innovate and eventually succumb to stagnation.

So while China undoubtedly will be a large and important player on the world stage for the next fifty years, it is very unlikely to maintain its current trajectory so long as it remains a dictatorial system. Long-term planning is definitely superior to the short-termism inherent in all modern representative democracies with their fickle electorates and their sensation-driven mass media, but the problem with long-term planning is that reality always ends up in a different place from where you thought it was going to be and so your plans don't coincide with what's now required. You can be lucky for a while, but no central planner remains lucky indefinitely. Even more importantly, in a top-down system apparatchiks compete for influence and spoils, which leads to inefficient allocation of resources which ultimately degrades the economy and leads to ever-more-desperate internal battles for whatever assets remain. The man at the top of the heap must act in ever more brutal ways in order to protect his own position, until finally all is chaos and death.

China's leadership does not yet seek to control every aspect of economic life, but it does control a great deal. Many companies are effectively under state control, the Communist Party determines investment priorities and infrastructure development and all the rules that govern everyday life. It is inevitable that under President Xi the Party will become ever more repressive as it seeks to control ever more thoroughly a population it fundamentally distrusts. This in turn will crush the life out of the Chinese economy until it becomes little more than Russia writ large. And that is a dismal fate indeed.

Tyranny therefore is not a replacement for democracy but merely an unpleasant distraction. People who think we should adopt "the Chinese Model" as a solution to our current problems are as foolish as those who think we should return to the Wild West.

If we stop confusing ourselves with purposeless comparisons between nations practicing representative democracy and nations utilizing other forms of government, we can look at the systemic problems inherent in representative democracy and understand a little better why so many developed countries today are committing social and economic suicide by electing representatives whose policies are guaranteed to destroy all the accomplishments of the last eighty years. We need to understand this phenomenon because it is crippling our ability to act with even a modicum of intelligence. And if we can't govern ourselves adequately and act wisely we have very little prospect of tackling the big issues that now confront us.

We are altering the planet in a great many ways through large-scale application of technology. The climate is changing significantly. We are denuding the oceans and exterminating entire ecosystems. We are destroying tropical forests and our methods of agriculture are poisoning rivers and lakes as well as stripping the soil of key nutrients and filling the atmosphere with greenhouse gasses. Few of these issues can be tackled successfully without international cooperation. But how can nations cooperate if the very systems of government they employ lead to factionalism, fractious citizens, and short-sighted policies designed not to serve the people wisely but to ensure re-election of the politicians proposing them? We cannot begin to address global issues when a significant percentage of the population votes for politicians promising simple-minded tribe-oriented "solutions" that utterly ignore the real issues we face and instead promote the idea that all will be well provided we can return to some mythical past in which everything was better for the dominant group.

As a species we are not going to get any smarter, nor any better-informed. We will remain intellectually limited, and limited also by our evolved behaviors such as those that preclude the abandonment of old beliefs when new facts are discovered. We will, in short, remain a species almost entirely unfit to confront the problems we've created in consequence of our tool-making ability. A tiny number of clever people have empowered the rest of us, and we're using that technological empowerment precisely as one might expect: we're ruining everything around us while we focus on meaningless squabbles and create ever-more-pointless social divisions.

Therefore the question of how to achieve adequate governance is vital and our answers to this question will ultimately have global significance.

Any reasonable person looking at the state of the world today would need to consume significant quantities of alcohol or narcotic in order to be able to draw the conclusion that we're shuffling along adequately and that all will somehow work out for the best. Each new election throws up ever-more-inadequate buffoons whose populist policies are then even more ruinous.

Why do we vote for charlatans, buffoons, and demagogues? Why do we seem unable to resist even the most simple-minded lies and absurdly impossible promises? To understand this curious phenomenon we need to stroll backward in time, to before the last ice-age and therefore before the development of agriculture, fixed settlements, and complex societies.

Our species and its progenitors evolved in conditions of relative simplicity. We had to make shelters, we had to find food, and we had to avoid being eaten by creatures that were faster and more powerful than ourselves. Over hundreds of thousands of years we gradually learned how to sharpen flint, harden wooden spears, and grunt in ways that were intelligible to each other. Much more significantly, through some chance genetic changes, we learned to imagine things. While it used to be believed that humans are different from other animals because we have opposing thumbs or large brains or the capacity for speech, the most striking difference between humans and all other animals is that we live predominantly in a world of imagination whereas other creatures live entirely in the real world. This is both our great strength and our great weakness.

So we imagined means of exchange such as conch-shells, beads, and other items that have no intrinsic worth but which can be imbued with great symbolic value. We imagined mommy gods and daddy gods who were just like us, only bigger and stronger. And so we could gather in groups bound together not merely by a network of inter-dependencies and reciprocal favors but by symbolic ties. These groups could become far larger than the size of any one tribe and ultimately such large groups enabled us to out-compete our other *homo* competitors and drive them to extinction.

We didn't triumph over homo Neanderthals or the Denisovians or any other human species because we had larger brains (in fact Neanderthals had larger brains than ours); we did so because we could amass much larger numbers on the battlefield in consequence sharing the same fantasy.

In short, we triumphed because we're pretty awful at dealing with reality but rather excellent at living in a fantasy world of our own making. Our fantasy worlds, however, aren't very complicated. This is because there's never been in our history as a species any evolutionary pressure on us to develop the capacity for complex thought. Anyone who doubts this can open any history book for any period and read a few pages; this will be sufficient to dispel any misconceptions about our cognitive capacity. We are very bad indeed at thinking ahead and have almost no capacity whatsoever for consistency-checking. To put it another way, if you believe A and you also believe B but A and B are mutually incompatible, you'll have no trouble at all maintaining both beliefs. Our brains are simply not hardwired to notice the incompatibility.

At this point you may be excused for thinking, "that's nonsense." So let's look at an example. The USA is the most superstitious economically developed nation in the world; its rate of religiosity is far higher than in all other Western nations. So it is quite common to hear educated Americans claiming that they understand evolutionary theory while at the same time possessing deep religious belief. Clearly these two positions are entirely incompatible, yet that doesn't stop millions of people from holding them in tandem. If educated Americans can provide this example, it's obvious that the average person is going to have no problem at all believing in all manner of mutually contradictory notions. This creates a significant problem when it comes to governance because we fare very poorly when it comes to assessing proposed policy.

Even when it comes to basic propositions, a great many people have no capacity to reason from them. Brexit provides a baleful example. Brexiteers may be dimly aware that as of 2016 forty-seven percent of the UK's gross domestic product was reliant on friction-free trade with the other twenty-seven European Union member nations. Yet at the same time Brexiteers also believe that the UK can leave the EU without suffering any harmful economic effects whatsoever. If people can't draw obvious conclusions from simple data, what chance is there that they can reason successfully about any aspect of our complex modern world?

We are not in fact "wise people" but instead a simple primate species the brains of which are adapted for the challenges of the African savanna and the primordial forests of Eurasia. We're quite literally cave people in a modern world. We evolved under conditions of scarcity in which every calorie was precious. As the human brain can consume more than thirty percent of a person's blood glucose through mental activity, quite naturally we evolved to do as little thinking as possible. Back on the savanna this was a perfectly viable strategy. Just do whatever you're told by a purported authority figure and for the most part all will be well, especially if he has an impressive bird-feather in his hair or an animal tooth on a string around his neck.

And when all was not well and an entire tribe succumbed to the consequences of their stupidity, this had negligible impact on the evolution of our species as a whole. Other tribes survived and carried the "let's not think about this" strategy forward. Simple problems generally could be solved with simple answers, so that's what our brains evolved to prefer.

Unfortunately for us our technologies, developed over centuries by a tiny number of atypically clever people, have radically altered the world we now inhabit. Most of us are not clever at all. We are ignorant savages stroking our smartphones and Kalashnikovs and our folly is destroying everything around us. Simple-minded answers to complex questions lead us ever further into disaster.

And that's why, to answer the question posed several paragraphs earlier, we reliably reject the competent in favor of the foolish. The foolish promise simple solutions to complex problems whereas the competent confuse us with facts and difficult-to-understand proposals. Simplistic "solutions" enable us to avoid learning facts, avoid grappling with cause-and-effect, and avoid struggling to see whether or not a proposed strategy could actually work under the circumstances that pertain. Far nicer for us to embrace uncritically a sound-bite that's easy for our little brains to grab hold of. We absorb the sound-bite, we adore its simplicity, and we vote for the buffoon who so kindly provided it to us.

And that, folks, is democracy.

Democracy has been stumbling along for over two hundred years during which its failings were disguised because the average person was unable to see it in operation. Distance and lack of communication technologies ensured that government was something that happened far away in a mysterious way. Things happened and as always they seemed inevitable, particularly when viewed in the rear-view mirror of history or through the lens of magical forces. For some people, it's always "god's will" that makes things happen; for others it is "economic determinism" and the grand sweep of historical inevitability. Some subscribe to the "great man" notion whereby one uber-individual emerges from the tumult of events and imposes his magnificent will, thereby fulfilling his "historical destiny." Most people simply tell themselves "everything happens for a reason" or "it was meant to be."

So people continue to be people and we bumble along ignorant, complacent, and utterly unaware of the possibility that there could be more adequate ways of doing things. We lurch from one unnecessary disaster to the next, led by glib-tongued amateurs who have little or no grasp of the problems they're trying to deal with and the rest of us try to get on with our lives as best as possible. For the most part life appears to operate in slow motion. A bad decision taken last year may not have any impact until next year; meanwhile crops have to be tended, managers assuaged, children chastised, lovers met in secluded locations, and illnesses to be endured. Few of us notice the cause-and-effect chains created by atrociously inept decision-making at the top of the hierarchy. In the past this bumbling-through was awful but usually not absolutely catastrophic except for all those millions who died in famines and wars. As history is written only by those who survive, the general attitude was, "well, that was a bit rough but look, we got through it so everything must be alright!" People continued to project their illusions of competence onto those at the top of the hierarchy, because that's what we humans do.

Today the situation is profoundly different. Instantaneous communication means the business of government is no longer performed at a distance. The mass media's need for continuous sensation and scandal to boost the value of advertising slots means that the "news" has become merely another branch of the entertainment industry. The consequence is that the average citizen is now aware of how inept politicians really are, but the blame remains personal rather than systemic. Individual politicians are held up for ridicule and censure but few bother to wonder why so many examples of incompetence are so readily brought to light.

As communications technologies have brought politicians and voters closer and closer together, politicians have reacted by attempting to promote even more policies they hope will appeal to the average citizen. But how well informed is the average citizen? On what basis does the famous "man in the street" assess such proposed policy? The British comedian Ricky Gervais commented a while back, "I hate it when a television news reporter says, 'and now let's hear what the man in the street thinks.' The man in the street is an idiot. I don't care what he thinks." We can note that Gervais' use of the word "idiot" is appropriate, for its Greek root means "a person who takes no interest in important matters of polity."

The problem at the heart of representative democracy is that we, the people, are in general even more intellectually incompetent and ignorant than those we vote for. As we watch our civilization collapse around us in a series of unedifying debacles we have only ourselves to blame.

This does not mean, however, that we can save ourselves by embarking on a global self-help binge. No amount of reading *The Seven Habits of Highly Competent Voters,* were such a book ever to be written, will obviate the fact that our brains are hardwired to prefer simple to complex and thus stupid to clever. What we need is not to pretend we can all become more adequately informed and rational citizens but rather to realize we need to create systems of governance that compensate for our profound shortcomings.

This may sound an impossible task but in fact it's commonplace. When we stroke our smartphones we're benefiting from the efforts of clever engineers to make something incredibly complex that nevertheless can be used by people who have no clue whatsoever about how it all works under the covers. When we drive our cars we likewise rely on the efforts of engineers to save us from our own incompetence. Today airbags and crumple zones and lane-departure management and collision avoidance systems and automated parking systems all utilize incredible complexity to make our individual actions as simple as possible. Even something as trivial as pressing the accelerator pedal to make the vehicle go faster involves hundreds of complex interactions, all disguised by engineers to seem simple to us as we drive along with our minds firmly focused on the latest trivial media scandal.

As engineers learn how people make a mess of things, they gradually design in systems that preclude or compensate for our incompetence. But we don't engineer our systems of governance.

Winston Churchill famously defended democracy as "the worst form of government except for all the other forms that have from time to time been tried" and apparently we're supposed to leave it at that. But we would be very discontent indeed if our National Airways pilot (who is only in left seat because she persuaded others that she'd be a "naturally great" pilot who would "make flying great again") told us as we were plummeting from the skies that "this is the worst form of air travel except for all the other forms of air travel that have from time to time been tried." How many of us would be thrilled to be offered, at great expense, an automobile that had no seatbelts, no airbags, only a wooden block as a brake, no windscreen wipers, a manual starting-crank, and a nice rubber bulb we have to squeeze every second in order to introduce petrol into the cylinders? Would we love this contraption merely because the salesperson assured us that it's better than all other forms of non-horse transportation that have from time to time been tried?

In short, our failure to innovate and improve our systems of government is shocking when put into context. It's as if we should be content to have in every kitchen, along with all our modern conveniences, four-year-old child-slaves using pestles and mortars to pound wheat kernels into flour.

Today's cheap quartz wristwatch is accurate to around one second per year whereas the most expensive wristwatch in the world sixty years ago was accurate to a few minutes per month. Today's modes of transportation are unimaginably safe and luxurious compared to what was available fifty years ago. And today's entertainments are far beyond anything imagined even twenty-five years ago. All of these improvements have come from engineers looking at what works, what doesn't work, and striving to make continuous improvements.

In the political realm we bumble on complacently, yet politics is far more important than seeing some ephemeral pop personality in high-definition on a tablet in order to idle away a few moments of life. Politics changes the destiny of millions. We've put enormous effort into delivering ephemera and zero effort into improving the way we govern ourselves. Are we really so stupid?

Well, actually... yes. Yes we are.

Here's the thing: we measure intellect by means of the IQ score. By definition the average score is 100 and equally by definition half the population therefore has an IQ of 100 or less. Sometimes a lot less. Now you'd think that this would be balanced out by the other half of the population having an IQ of 100 and above. Sadly, such optimism would be unwarranted. It does not take much to score above 100. The more telling metric is that only fourteen percent of the population has an IQ above 115 and this score is not a particularly demanding benchmark. Back in the days when the most complicated task we'd have to master would be how high to fill the milk bucket or how many lumps of coal to put on the fire, it didn't matter that most of us are a bit thick. Today however it really does matter. A lot. And even those few of us who are capable of more sophisticated intellectual processes rarely bother to expend the time and effort required to become familiar with the various policy proposals proffered by the political Parties. Only a tiny handful of citizens are both intelligent and informed and as we shall see later, these voters are entirely ignored.

Once we got ourselves locked into the notion of representative democracy it was inevitable that the franchise would expand. People with votes inevitably voted for politicians promoting policies that intentionally or otherwise discriminated against people without the vote. The only way to attempt to assure a more equitable state of affairs, short of killing everyone in politics and starting all over again, was to extend the franchise. Eventually even women were given the vote and sure enough, discriminatory policies slowly began to ebb away in favor of less biased laws and customs. Society gradually became more egalitarian. And that was a Very Good Thing.

Unfortunately the notion of matching responsibilities to rights was utterly ignored. Whereas you need to pass at least a rudimentary driving test to be permitted to drive, and a more rigorous series of tests if you wish to fly an aircraft or pilot a ship, and achieve an even higher standard of competence if you wish to make your living as a dentist or a surgeon or an engineer, there is absolutely no qualification required if you want to vote and thereby influence the fate of your nation. All you have to do is keep living until you reach the "age of majority." At that point you can be an inebriated moron who thinks the world is flat and that the moon is made of cheese and yet your vote will count for just as much as a thoughtful citizen who takes the time and expends the effort to be informed about real-world facts and who reasons carefully from them.

This is why the humorist H. L. Mencken wrote, "Democracy is the pathetic belief in collective wisdom emerging from individual ignorance."

At this point it is traditional, if not actually mandatory, to utter cries of condemnation. We are all equal! Everyone must have the right to vote! *Aux barricades, citoyens!*

Except of course we are not all equal. Some of us are short, some are tall. Some are blessed with good looks while the rest of us must make do with envy. Talent is distributed very unequally. That's why we're not all pilots or surgeons or musicians or chess Grand Masters. It's no good shouting that everyone is as good as everyone else because that just makes us hypocrites. When our teeth hurt we go to a qualified dentist; we don't ask Joe from next door if he'd like to try his hand at root canal surgery. If we're unfortunate enough to have a brain tumor we hope for the best neurosurgeon possible; we certainly don't hand a scalpel to Suzy who, between binge-watching back episodes of Star Trek Next Money-Spinning Iteration, keeps harping on about being "the greatest" neurosurgeon despite knowing nothing whatsoever about neurosurgery and being the less-than-proud possessor of a rather unfortunate involuntary-but-honestly-my-dear-hardly-noticeable-at-all hand spasm.

Drawing closer, how many people do you know who are genuinely well-informed about even a fraction of the key issues of the day and who reason persistently from real-world facts? As the vast majority of us merely repeat Internet memes and sound-bites, chances are that unless you interpret the above criteria very generously indeed, you don't know many people who ought to be trusted with a vote. Yet we give the vote to everyone over the age of majority.

This apparently minor oversight is the reason the world is being subsumed by a wave of mindless populism upon which a motley and unsavory group of wannabe demagogues are surfing to power. Populism exists because we've failed to realize that we are the authors of our own misfortunes. We blame variously "the elites" (whoever they are supposed to be, but we'll come to that later) and we never look in the mirror to see where the real blame lies. It lies with us because we're all a bit thick. But we're so used to being simple-minded that we don't notice. In fact, the more stupid and ignorant we are, the more we're convinced that we're smart and capable. We don't know what we don't know and so we live in a comfortable cocoon of folly, never once glimpsing the larger reality beyond our reach.

We fail to notice many obvious things, one example being that if we use age as the criterion for being permitted to vote, we'll tend to elect politicians who promote policies that discriminate against the young and the unborn. These people are our children and grand-children so we really ought to care. But we are so clueless we don't even realize what we're doing.

Here's our situation: canny politicians realized some time ago that most of us don't pay much attention to what's going on. We just want free ice-cream forever. The fact that there's no such thing as free ice-cream forever is an unfortunate fact of life, but luckily it's a fact that can be dodged for a considerable period of time. So politicians promise us free ice-cream and they pay for it by borrowing. No rich nation has run a balanced budget (where expenditures are not greater than tax income) for decades now. Every developed nation is in debt. The money has been spent on buying all that free ice-cream that makes us, if not happy, then at least a bit less discontent than we'd otherwise be.

Who pays for the debt? Ah! That's the magical part! Remember how we have age as our sole criterion for being permitted to vote? Well, those too young (or too unborn) to vote are the ones who will get stuck with the bill. We spend the money, our children and grand-children pick up the tab. What could be more splendid than this? It really is one of the major triumphs of democracy.

On the very rare occasion that someone tries to point out this rather dubious game of pass-the-debt-parcel, politicians and a few tame economists retort that debt isn't a problem because we will grow our way out of it as gross domestic product (GDP) expands. This however is fallacious because since World War II we've lived through the greatest expansion of GDP in history and debt has increased. Even worse, as GDP numbers improve, governments borrow even more money as a result. The hard fact is that we've condemned our children and grand-children to a far worse standard of living than our own because we spent what we inherited from our parents and we're spending the inheritance of our descendants simply because they aren't here to vote for policies that would be less inequitable.

It addition we're destroying the planet they will have to live on. Global warming, denuding the oceans, and burning down forests are all examples of short-term profit-seeking at the expense of future generations. Our children and grand-children will truly have many reasons to hate us for what we've bequeathed to them. A few people appear to believe that we should zoom off to Mars to "save humanity" but a moment's thought reveals this to be merely simple-mindedness with a few toys thrown into the mix, nothing more than a billionaire's panic room built on another planet. We depend upon millions of complex interactions in a world we're evolved to fit into. The notion that we can destroy the Earth but blithely live on under an artificial dome thirty-six million miles away on a dead world is merely an illustration of how intellectual ability in one domain (for example, persuading investors to part with billions of dollars to fund grandiose schemes) does not necessarily translate into another. We need to stop being careless of the harm we're inflicting, not pretend we can blast off to Plan(et) B and live happily ever after.

Now we need to look at one more area in which representative democracy discriminates against a certain segment of society: the thoughtful.

A long, long time ago, back in the distant mists of time (well, 1952 to be precise), perhaps the most able and intelligent candidate in the history of the United States was running for President. This man's name was Adlai Stevenson. He made a thoughtful, insightful, and coherent speech after which an acolyte congratulated him with the words, "Mister Stevenson, after hearing that speech every thinking man and woman in America will vote for you!" To which Stevenson, a realist if ever there was one, replied, "Thank you, but I need a majority to win."

Stevenson understood that most people either don't have the intellectual capacity to engage with difficult topics or they lack the interest to do so. Whichever the case, it is always true everywhere and at every time that only a tiny minority of voters actually understands the issues of the day and can reach rational conclusions about them. Most people just want simple-minded sound-bites that make them feel good.

While it is obvious that most politicians aren't very bright it is also obvious that successful politicians do know a thing or two about politics. And the first thing that must be known if you're an aspiring politician is that you have limited resources. Therefore you must use these resources wisely. So you cast your jaundiced and baleful eye across the vast swathe of electorate. You observe that a significant number of people are willing to take whatever you say at face value provided you say it using monosyllabic words and speak slowly. Even better if you can smile and crack a joke; politics is, after all, a branch of the entertainment industry.

The great thing about most people is that once they've decided they like you, they will stick with you regardless of whatever happens next. It's just easier that way. Research shows that once we believe something to be true ("he's a great man, he'll make our country great again") we ignore and deny any real-world evidence that contradicts our beliefs. In fact the more the evidence shows we're wrong, the stronger we hold on to our beliefs and the more we hate those who are inconsiderate enough to point out that our beliefs are sadly unsupported by reality. This is why, for example, even after every single Brexit promise was shown to be a lie, Brexiteers continued to support the UK leaving the European Union and thus inflicting upon the country they claim to love the greatest national self-harm project in history. Once we believe something, we reject reality in order to preserve our beliefs. This is what it means to be human.

If we didn't behave like this we'd be forced to grapple with facts, we'd have to expend mental effort attempting to reconcile previous belief with current evidence, and we might even have to admit we were wrong in our original belief. This is why a majority of Russians today still think Stalin was a "great" leader rather than a psychotic moron and why a similar majority of Chinese still think Mao was a "great helmsman" rather than a psychotic moron. In the USA today some forty-three million people believe fervently in a blabbering infantile orange moron whose primary claims to fame are (a) the astonishing ability to lose money owning a casino, and (b) hosting a trash television show in which he bullied hapless underlings in obedience to a script written by other people.

There are a great many more examples to choose from but these are sufficient to show rather conclusively that we humans aren't very good at spotting the blindingly obvious. We then compound our errors by refusing to acknowledge reality.

So all politicians realize, sooner or later, that they should expend their limited resources on capturing a reliable bloc of voters and the most reliable are those who can't be bothered to think much about the issues. Emotion wins over reason, so trot out some platitudes, whip people up into a frenzy of resentment against some notional enemy, and you get the votes you need. Best of all, those people will keep voting for you for years and years, simply because it becomes a habit. A significant number of US citizens voted for Trump, despite loathing him, merely because he was the Republican candidate. It didn't matter that Trump repudiated all Republican policies and was quite evidently an incompetent narcissist; people who vote the Republican ticket will always vote the Republican ticket regardless of the candidate. They just can't help themselves. As any cigarette-smoker knows, once you form a habit it's nearly impossible to break.

So what about the small minority of citizens who are thoughtful and who expend the effort required to understand the important issues of the day? Every successful politician on the planet knows to ignore these people. They're just time-wasters. There are too few of them to matter and they wouldn't repay the effort required to woo them. They would ask awkward questions and when new information becomes available they might change their minds.

In short, the intelligent and well-informed are just not worth the effort.

So in a representative democracy, politicians get elected by pandering to those who are easily swayed by empty bluster and emotional manipulation. In a representative democracy the thoughtful and informed are, to all intents and purposes, disenfranchised. It's a beautiful system, isn't it?

The US Republican politician Bobby Jindal is a highly instructive example of how aiming very low turns out to be the ideal strategy in a democracy. In the first decade of the twenty-first century Jindal was on record as lamenting the fact that the Republican Party had very obviously become "the Stupid Party." He exhorted his fellow Republicans to abjure foolish non-solutions and instead raise the tone of debate and increase the coherence of the Party's various policies. Jindal clearly had failed to understand the inner logic of Republican strategy since the days of Richard Nixon and likewise failed to grasp how powerful a strategy it was. After the victory of Donald Trump, Jindal realized the error of his ways and went on record saying that the Republican Party needed to avoid the trap of not being stupid enough.

Whichever way you look at it, aside from the perspective of self-immolating satire, representative democracy is not only unfit for purpose but also rather immoral. Which is not quite the shining example it's claimed to be.

The Coming Storm

If representative democracy is a shambles then what will happen next? As best as we can tell, Plato's critique of democracy is coming true. He pointed out that democracy means anyone who can persuade a sufficient percentage of the population to rally behind him will end up leading a mob and this will ultimately result in the establishment of a tyranny.

Today we see that the shelf-life of representative democracy has expired and things are beginning to rot. Everywhere we look populism is taking hold and people are pointing at one another and shouting "enemy!"

To understand why we're being such simpletons we have to go back in time once again. Humans evolved in relatively small groups, perhaps no more than one hundred and fifty individuals. That's about the limit of the human brain's capacity to remember the complex web of favors owed and owing, who's on the way up and who's on the way down, who may be a good ally tomorrow and who is likely to betray us as soon as they get a chance.

Each small group would inevitably from time to time come into conflict with other groups. Survival therefore meant having a strong sense of us-versus-them. *They* were by definition Bad and *we* were by definition the personification of every imaginable virtue. This polarizing mentality kept the group together and enabled it to marshal its forces when confronted by another group. Although today we live in much larger social organizations and although our world is infinitely more subtle and complex, our brains are still firmly hardwired for us-versus-them.

This makes it very easy for a wannabe demagogue to manipulate our emotions by creating the conditions in which we come to believe we're being threatened by people who are not *us*. The more frightened and angry we are, the more our already-slender capacity for reason is inhibited.

History tells us that once you work enough people up into enough of a state there's no turning back. Fear, suspicion, and sheer bloody-minded stupidity are corrosive. Like acid eating through the supporting girders of a skyscraper, once a certain amount of damage has been done the ultimate collapse of the structure is inevitable no matter how hard we may try to patch things up in the interim.

It's not easy for us to imagine a future that is significantly different from today. Major political upheavals seem to occur in slow-motion to those who live through them. Very few people understood that Hitler's appointment as Chancellor would change Europe forever. The day after his appointment the sun rose as usual, people went to work as usual, the shops opened as usual, and all the thousand-and-one quotidian events took place just as they had the day before. Yet we know with hindsight that the fragile veneer of civilization would be unpeeled with astonishing rapidity: within a mere six years the world would be at war.

The same is true today. Our thin veneer of civilization appears to us as inevitable, so we fail to protect it. Instead we applaud entertaining blusterers whose only contribution to civilization is to weaken it. We vote for incompetents and halfwits with the same degree of forethought we give to voting for competitors on televised talent shows. No doubt there's a certain satisfaction in voting for people who seem to be "just like us" but that transient pleasure will be paid for by our children whose lives will be irredeemably blighted.

Yes, this is a rather dark and gloomy prognosis. Surely in a world of streaming video and supposed "citizen journalism" such horrors as the gulags and the concentration camps are impossible? Surely we're too civilized to permit a repetition?

It's salutary to remember that Germany was the most civilized nation on Earth in the early part of the twentieth century. Germany was the first to provide social security benefits to all citizens; its educational system was far ahead of its peers; quality of life was very high for the time; and learning was valued. None of this stopped the eruption of two catastrophic World Wars in which over one hundred million people perished and many more had their lives scarred forever.

Oh, and yes, Germany was a democracy, as were most of the other combatant nations. So much for the notion that democracy confers stability.

Turning from the past to the present, what do we see? The USA has long been a rogue actor, using its economic might to impose its will and sometimes to start unnecessary wars in order to benefit its large corporations. The CIA has a long and brutal history of deposing elected politicians in order to install "friendly" right-wing dictatorships and deploying its military might to prop up existing right-wing dictatorships. Many of these actions were purportedly to prevent the expansion of Soviet influence and today similar actions are defended on the grounds of being part of the "war on terror." By amazing coincidence US corporations also happen to reap substantial economic benefits from these actions.

Therefore citing the USA as a pillar of peaceful democracy and a primary guarantor of the rule of law isn't quite as reassuring as some people would like to pretend. Lest anyone has forgotten, after the events of 11th September 2001 that were perpetrated by the al Qaida network operating out of Afghanistan, the USA went on to invade Iraq which was a country that had absolutely nothing whatsoever to do with 9/11 but which did represent "unfinished business" for the Bush family, a scion of which happened to occupy the White House at the time. If such harm can be perpetrated on such slender grounds merely because a dull-witted individual by chance (or in this case, by Supreme Court edict) happens to be in a position of power, it's obvious that democracy isn't worth much.

Europe has been more circumspect. After the ravages of two World Wars, the Western European powers have largely focused on domestic policies and trade-based prosperity. Today however Europe is succumbing to the same populist-nationalist frenzy that is destroying many other regions. Unscrupulous politicians and other dullards have embraced with great enthusiasm the realization that the mob is easily duped and that the simplest way to reap votes is to appeal to our worst instincts. Brexit and Trump showed the world that even the most infantile and pathetically obvious lies will triumph over facts and reason.

Why did simpletons telling simple-minded lies gain such easy victories? Aren't we proud of the fact nearly every citizen completes secondary education these days and therefore, supposedly, is capable of making more informed decisions?

23

To see why this notion is barren, let's consider the question of *trade*.

Trade is difficult for our primate brains to understand. In the environment we evolved in, we had to be suspicious of the other side. Is that piece of meat really worth three whole bananas? Even after the agricultural revolution and the widespread use of symbolic exchange known as "money" it was still easy for people to cheat. As recently as the eighteenth century, people still clipped coins and we've never stopped arguing over what constitutes a "fair" rate of exchange. Although prices are now bar-coded and you can't clip a credit card, we've only outsourced our disagreements to professional hagglers. Oddly it's usually the world's most powerful economy that in paranoid (and ignorant) fashion imagines that other nations are "manipulating" their currencies to "rip off" the good ol' US of A. Back in the 1970s Japan was in the dock; over the last few years various US politicians have claimed that China is a "currency manipulator." As always, facts and reason have no purchase whereas empty assertions and "patriotic" emotions dominate.

We take all the benefits of markets for granted and we fixate on the small number of problems they cause. Few sights are more revealing of our inherent mental limitations than watching earnest citizens protesting against global trade while sipping lattes that exist only because of global trade, wearing clothes that exist only because of global trade, and organizing themselves via smartphones that exist only because of global trade.

Now there certainly are objections to the various systems of global trade we presently experience. Firstly, inadequate government regulation and enforcement can mean that monopolies or consortia can come into existence and manipulate the system to their advantage. This is why, for example, growers of commodity products such as coffee often find themselves paid very little for their crops while intermediaries enjoy much larger margins. The solution is not, as per US and EU government policies, to subsidize growers but rather to remove the regulatory distortions that have caused the problem in the first place.

But acting intelligently is very different from acting in knee-jerk fashion while mouthing incoherent nonsense about "balanced trade" and "fairness." Knee-jerk reactions that appeal to simple-minded notions of "fairness" almost always lead to self-harm.

To take a recent example: if China wants to subsidize the price of steel by using its taxpayers' money to provide steel more cheaply than is possible in the more developed nations, importing nations should be very happy indeed because they're essentially being given a gift. Cheaper steel brings down the cost of automobiles, buildings and bridges, refrigerators, and indeed anything that utilizes steel as an input. The Trump tariff duties on Chinese steel merely drive up the cost of US automobiles, refrigerators, and infrastructure. Although Trump supporters think this is "smart," more intellectually competent people can see it's rather foolish to harm one's own people merely because someone else is trying to give them a gift of cheap steel. Although a few thousand US steel jobs may be lost by accepting subsidized imports, tens of thousands of other jobs will be created. It's a net win for the USA if the Chinese government wants to subsidize steel. Furthermore, although Trump may lie blatantly and proclaim that China will pay the cost of tariffs, the reality is that US corporations actually pay the tariffs. Which means, ultimately, that Trump voters are supporting a policy that requires them to pay an estimated $1,300 in unnecessary costs for every single person in the country. Trump voters remain unperturbed, however, because like most voters they are ignorant of reality. Our primate brains are hardwired to understand us-versus-them but largely incapable of dealing with the complexities of our modern interdependent world. And as always we accept mindless assertion instead of taking the time to uncover the truth.

The hard fact is, as a species we're just not able to understand the world we live in and so we harm the very things we depend on. Only by recognizing our hardwired mental limitations can we ever hope to circumvent them. Otherwise we'll remain trapped in a mire of simplistic emotional responses to complex problems that properly require facts and reason to address.

Today we are very far from any conception of our limitations. Instead we're in the midst of simple-minded nonsense that will tear our civilization apart. One very popular cry is that "the will of the people" should be paramount. This particular sound-bite is especially pernicious because if you don't think about it (and who thinks about anything?) it seems perfectly reasonable. What could be more democratic than the triumph of "the will of the people?"

The problem is, of course, that there's no such thing as "the will of the people." Take any group and you'll find dozens of different desires, beliefs, and political postures. It is ludicrous to claim that an entire nation, or even merely a slender majority of its citizens, has a single opinion on anything. Even at the individual level, people are a confused mass of often contradictory desires. For example, "I want to eat that slice of pie" and "I want to lose weight by dieting" are not uncommon desires found within a single person. Likewise at the national level people often support policies that will achieve the precise opposite of what they believe. Not only is the concept of "the will of the people" utterly meaningless but also it doesn't matter what people want if it's not possible to provide it. Many people want things that are completely beyond reach.

Furthermore, even if it were possible to arrive at a single "will of the people" why do we think that would be worth considering? Remember, eighty-six percent of the population lacks the cognitive ability to reason with any degree of competence, and of the fourteen percent who surmount the hurdle very few can bother to become informed about the facts pertaining to our major real-world problems. If it were magically possible to know "the will of the people" the overwhelming probability is that will would be hopelessly ignorant and foolish.

On the few occasions where anything remotely resembling "the will of the people" existed, that will was indeed profoundly misguided. For example, from the late 1950s to the mid-1970s, the UK repeatedly sought to challenge Iceland's right to restrict fishing within its territorial waters. The UK population, whipped up by the print media, was outraged. Thousands of British fishing jobs were at stake, as was the British right to cheap cod! The "will of the people" in this instance was clear: the UK should have every right to over-fish Icelandic waters regardless of the catastrophic consequences this would have on the cod population. The UK government, eager to appease its "patriotic" citizens, sent warships to escort British commercial fishing vessels. Iceland deployed its fleet to restrict British access. Each of these so-called "cod wars" ended up in international mediation where the Icelandic position was judged by intelligent and informed people to be far more reasonable and sensible than the British position, which was essentially "we want free ice-cream forever and damn the consequences!" Had the British "will of the people" prevailed, as similar "wills" did sadly prevail in places such as the fishing grounds off the north-east coast of the United States, cod stocks would have collapsed entirely. The hard fact is that the vast majority of people aren't very clever and don't understand complex issues. Bowing to the "will of the people" therefore, on the few occasions when such a thing may even be said to exist, will always result in catastrophically poor outcomes.

"The will of the people" is therefore nothing more than an empty slogan employed by those seeking to rise to power on the back of a slogan-chanting mob. No doubt we shall hear this phrase a great deal in the years to come as a small army of chancers, opportunists, and thugs jostle for prominence as our civilization collapses into disarray.

It seems we're doomed to tear apart our civilization, allow halfwits and rogues to ascend to power, wreck our economies and the world around us, and then blame the predictably catastrophic results on someone else. Brexit is a classic example of what occurs when simple-minded lies propel an entire nation down a one-way path to enormous self-harm. Only a handful of British people will acknowledge that the entire mess is home-grown; a majority will blame the European Union for the inevitably catastrophic outcome simply because this is the easiest thing to do and requires no thinking whatsoever. There will be no shortage of venal politicians and gutter press seeking transient benefit who will encourage the populace in this mistaken belief. And this, ladies and gentlemen, is what sows the seeds of future wars: lies, mistrust, and a deep sense of grievance.

Meanwhile the USA will travel even further down the road to becoming a medieval theocracy with modern weapons, the European Union will collapse, China will dominate its region while becoming ever more repressive at home, and Russia will rot while creating havoc all around itself. Ordinary people will be convinced by charlatans that everyone else is to blame for the deterioration and in such circumstances violent conflict is inevitable. The European Union was the greatest peace project known to humankind, and it's being torn apart by mindless populism.

We can expect the next fifty years to bring with them impoverishment, hatred, violence, further degradation of the planet, and an unimaginable amount of totally unnecessary harm. All because we're unable to get beyond our primate instincts and group-species limitations. Our capacity to make clever tools has dramatically out-stripped our capacity to use such tools wisely; we have quite literally put the means of mass destruction into the hands of idiots.

We can only hope that after such unnecessary suffering a few wise heads among the survivors will look around and say to themselves, "oh, let's not do that again." And so we need to look ahead and see, with whatever scraps of optimism we can stitch together, what better approaches to governance may be feasible.

Can We Fix It?

There are two basic categories of problem when it comes to things that aren't working as desired. The first category is where the fundamental predicates are such that any attempts to improve the original will fail because the basis on which the original was constructed cannot be modified sufficiently to meet our needs. For example: attempting powered flight by strapping wings onto your arms will lead to failure no matter how many clever alloys or carbon-fiber composites you may wish to try. With such problems the best thing to do is toss everything onto the rubbish heap and re-think things from first principles.

With consumer products, medical technologies, and military hardware there's a relentless process of evolution at work. Things that no longer work well enough to meet our needs are, after a time, scrapped and entirely new things replace them. These new things are then incrementally improved so that each generation of products is better than the last. And when incremental enhancement is no longer enough to meet the needs of the ecosystem, we throw out the old and start anew with something that more closely meets our new requirements. Jet engines replaced propellers, quartz replaced mechanical mechanisms in our wristwatches, petroleum products replaced coal as the primary fuel for transportation, and silicon chips replaced vacuum valves. And now these new technologies are incrementally improved in turn.

This is why our cars, phones, aircraft, and telescopes are all better today than they were even a decade ago.

The bad news is that representative democracy is like strapping wings onto your arms and believing you'll be able to fly. This is not entirely surprising given that, with the sole exception of the US Constitution, representative democracy wasn't designed. It grew haphazardly out of transient local conditions, morphing and adapting where possible but always limping badly because the fundamental concept was mistaken. To reiterate the problem: representative democracy can only function when (a) there is an informed and thoughtful citizenry, and (b) there is a competent and diligent set of representatives.

Which is more or less equivalent to saying that democracy can only be a success when (a) anti-gravity chewing gum exists, and (b) diamonds grow on trees.

It would be lovely if, fairytale-like, there was some great cosmic story-teller who could offer hope and reassurance. Many people favor this approach, saying things like "tyranny always fails in the end" and "truth and freedom always triumph in the end over lies and oppression."

Such statements would be somewhat more convincing if (a) they were factually true, and (b) hundreds of millions of lives weren't blighted irretrievably by lies and oppression for enormous periods of time.

A glance at history shows us an uncomfortable reality: for most of human history tyranny has been the dominant form of power under one guise or another. Billions of lives have been spent in their entirety under the heavy foot of an oppressor. If we're to avoid more centuries of misery and horror we must become conscious actors in our own drama, take the reins, and proceed in a direction we believe can result in better outcomes than can be achieved by mouthing platitudes, cheering the next great leader, and hoping for the best.

Carl Popper, in his seminal work *The Open Society and its Enemies*, argued that the question was not Plato's "who shall rule?" but rather "how best to ensure that bad rulers can be removed from power?" Under this dictum, representative democracy is clearly superior to all prior forms of governance. Unfortunately Popper's logic does not encompass the entire problem domain and by being incomplete thereby fails to address the core issue.

For all his failings as a philosopher, Plato at least framed the correct question. In his *Republic* Plato itemized the various weaknesses of democracy, correctly foresaw that democracy ultimately leads to tyranny, and argued that only a form of benevolent autocracy could provide long-term stability and rational policies. We can forgive Plato the blinkers he wore in consequence of his time and circumstance and acknowledge that his critique of democracy is still highly pertinent two and a half thousand years later, even if his solution is a non-starter. It is long past time that we returned to the question he posed.

So: who indeed shall rule? Representative democracy appears to answer the question by saying, "the people shall rule" but in reality what happens is that a small coterie of professional politicians comes into existence and is largely dependent upon not the citizenry as a whole but rather upon powerful special interest groups. This is because while the populace flits from media-driven sensation to media-driven sensation, special interest groups pursue their goals persistently and patiently over long periods of time and deploy money and personnel where they can be most effective. Inevitably this results in government policy being crafted to favor special interests rather than the more diffuse and complex interests of the nation as a whole. Although politicians find themselves forced to respond to media-driven crises from time to time, on the whole policy continues to favor those who are best placed to pay for it. By way of analogy, a parent will occasionally appease a shrieking toddler but will devote far more time and resources to satisfying on a regular basis the requirements of their employer. Today in the USA the vast majority of legislation is actually drafted by lobby groups and simply rubber-stamped by the Congress and the President. Not surprisingly therefore the vast majority of legislation favors the rich and the powerful at the expense of ordinary citizens.

In Western Europe pay-to-play is generally less overt but politicians long ago learned to appease those who can control their fates. Such people include media barons who can whip up the mob, and cliques of insiders who wield unseen but highly significant power that is always deployed to maintain their own interests.

So it's reasonable to ask: "How can we structure things so that governance can be in the interests of all rather than merely in the service of powerful special interests, and how shall power be constrained so that a relapse into capture by special interests is rendered unlikely?" Furthermore we must ask, "How can the interests of the all be adequately defined and fairly pursued when there are so many disparate and conflicting desires among the citizenry and citizens themselves are generally incapable of understanding and recognizing their own best interests?"

These are large problems, but unfortunately the problems of democracy don't end there. Just as there is no "will of the people" but instead an incalculable number of incompatible hopes, desires, wishes, and beliefs scattered among millions of folk, there are also very few individual citizens whose desires are actually congruent. For example in the United

Kingdom people want the National Health Service (NHS) to provide unlimited care to all who need it, yet don't want to pay higher taxes. Apparently the money is supposed to fall from the sky like magic. Worse yet, the average British citizen makes very poor lifestyle choices that result in chronic ailments that, you guessed it, sap the resources of the NHS and make the whole situation worse.

So if even at the level of the individual we don't find a rational and consistent set of desires, how on earth are we supposed to believe that representative democracy instantiates the rule of the people?

When Emmanuel Macron, looking to defuse the *manifestations* of the gilets jaunes, went off on his three-month peregrination around France and set up multiple websites to gather the wishes of the people, not surprisingly he found they were incoherent. French people want to save the planet but not have higher fuel prices that would act to reduce carbon emissions. French people want many more secure jobs but don't want the policies that would create those jobs. French people want more State aid but don't want to pay the taxes this would require. And so on, and on, and on. The fact is, the average person simply wants free ice-cream forever with no consequences. And that isn't possible. The more we indulge the fantasy that ordinary ignorant foolish people are competent to have a say in governance and must be pandered to, the more we head down the road to inevitable catastrophe.

Turning once again to Brexit, the author's favorite example of the incoherence of popular sentiment came from a Brexit supporter in Cardiff, Wales. This man was very clear about his motivation: "I voted for Brexit because I'm sick and tired of all those English coming to Wales and buying up our houses." Comment on this particular motivation would be superfluous.

Returning for a moment to Popper, he and a great many other observers of the social order also failed to see that democratic structures are extremely vulnerable to those who don't adhere to them. Someone uninhibited by moral or intellectual constraints may come to power democratically and thereafter undermine the democratic structure so as to achieve *de facto* dictatorship.

Furthermore, Popper could not have foreseen a world in which instantaneous global communications and the media's need for eyeball-grabbing sensation leads to a situation in which individual thought is paralyzed by a perpetual bombardment of horrific yet wildly misleading images and sound-bites. It's ironic that although today there is more information available than ever before, our individual ability to discern what matters and what is mere ephemera is much degraded. Today the average citizen resembles a prisoner perpetually subject to bright lights and loud noises, unable to sleep when tired and unable to focus thought when awake. It's not surprising that some very poor quality decisions occur when such citizens, dazed and confused by the perpetual media barrage, stumble into a voting booth.

Most people therefore end up voting for candidates whose positions are largely spurious and based entirely upon false premises, merely because a sound-bite appealed to their emotions.

Looking today at the emergence of *de facto* tyranny in the OECD nations, we see that among the many factors tipping the balance towards dictatorship-via-democracy is the fact that political Parties have become largely irrelevant.

In the good old days Parties attempted to encompass and consolidate a set of relatively homogenous interests and ambitious individuals rose through the Party system. This tended to temper any individual demagogue and subdue him or her largely to the norms of the Party. Today it is apparent that Parties have generally lost relevance. Demagogues appeal directly to the people. Party members will then eagerly prostrate themselves before whatever demagogue deigns to inscribe the Party name upon his coat-tails, regardless of what his professed policies or goals may happen to be. The demagogue scorns former Party values? Then away with old Party values! In this phenomenon we see the loss one of the key dampening factors that permitted representative democracy to lurch along for so long despite its many systemic flaws.

As the twenty-first century unfolds we are coming to understand that stable political Parties can only exist for as long as there are relatively obvious homogenous blocs of common interest through which a great many individuals can feel part of a meaningful group. In Britain during much of the 19th and 20th centuries such blocs were initially the laboring class and a much smaller capital-owning class whose interests were also generally (though imperfectly) aligned with a growing middle class. Each group promoted its own interests at the expense of the whole and for most of the twentieth century politics was a form of see-saw, with policy shifting from side to side based on who happened to gain a majority at the last Election. In countries such as Italy, Marxists on one side and Christian Democrats on the other represented the extremes of possibility; in the UK a less polarized version of this opposition was embodied in the Labour Party versus the Conservatives. In the USA a milquetoast version of this counterpoint was for decades embodied in the Republican Party (ostensibly representing the haves) and the Democrats (ostensibly representing the have-nots).

In the USA the counterpoint was less damaging as nearly everyone agreed most of the time on the general superiority of a free market system even though in practice the market was generally rigged in favor of the wealthy and in favor of major industries such as automobiles, coal, steel, aircraft, and agricultural staples. As always, the gains of the few were paid for by the losses of the many but the many failed to notice and so the distortions persisted undisturbed.

But as the two basic categories (haves versus have-nots) become less homogenous because of multiple independent factors, the cohesion of the Party system breaks down. Over time it becomes apparent that Parties no longer have much to offer the general population and at the same time the inherent cronyism and corruption becomes more evident as the media seeks ever-more-compelling scandals by means of which to attract eyeballs and thereby maximize the value of their advertising slots. As the media bombards the citizenry with endless tales of scandal and incompetence and as groups fragment and pursue ever-more-extreme and ever-more-conflicting objectives, anxiety and fear spread and people begin to yearn for a "strong" leader to save them from uncertainty.

We also yearn to belong to a strong group but the old-style political Parties no longer have much to offer us from a psychological perspective. At the same time we've fragmented our other social affiliations. We no longer work for one company our entire lives; now we move from company to company and thus those we work with change regularly too. We no longer live in one house our entire lives and thus our neighbors change regularly. We no longer have one or two private interests that we pursue for our entire lives; now we jump from hobby to hobby, often at the prompting of corporations that need us to discard yesterday's must-have distraction in favor of the latest greatest device or pastime. Under such conditions of flux it is not surprising that we should be dissatisfied with the old forms of affiliation while yearning for something to take their place. Into the void steps The Great Dictator in his various guises, offering the illusion of group membership in return for our unquestioning support.

Religious organizations often support such "strong men" as they press to the fore because religionists by definition crave simple answers and cling to a black-and-white worldview. The psyche of the believer is not well formed to cope with the world's complexities, which is why religionists embrace simplistic mythologies in order to find their "answers" and "guidance." Religious fervor and political fervor are identical: both have their creeds, dogmas, rituals, and black-and-white thinking. Many people forget that the Nazi Party's strongest supporters in 1930s Germany were German Catholics and German Protestants; both groups believed the "values" embodied by National Socialism were consonant with their own mythological beliefs.

The support of myth-based organizations frequently serves to cloak the inherent ugliness of dictatorial regimes and provides the ordinary citizen with an illusion of respectability even while the first horrors are being perpetrated. One perfectly appropriate slogan for the Roman Catholic Church could be "Proudly Supporting Tyrants since 382 AD" having embraced over the years a wide variety of unsavory Kings and Emperors and more recently Leaders and Parties including Mussolini's Fascists and Hitler's Nazi Party as well as several ultra-right-wing South American dictators and today it has embraced enthusiastically the neo-fascist PiS in Poland.

Lest the reader should feel we are unfairly singling out one particular myth-based organization it's pertinent to note that the Russian Orthodox Church has thrown its weight behind Putin's repressions and military adventures abroad, the Greek Orthodox Church tacitly supported the military coup in Greece in 1967, and Turkey's new Sultan Recep Tayyip Erdoğan derives much of his power from his close identification with increasingly repressive Islamism. India has turned down the dark one-way street of Hindu Nationalism, Pakistan has long fomented Islamic extremism under the insane delusion that this would destabilize its neighbor rather than itself, and Buddhists in Myanmar are enthusiastically exterminating the Rohinga. Rabble-rousing politicians in Indonesia, Brunei, and Malaysia are likewise encouraging, and being encouraged by, Islamic extremism. Meanwhile in the US Presidential election of 2016, over eighty-five percent of Evangelical Christians supported Donald Trump, a sexual predator, serial adulterer, compulsive liar, infantile halfwit and the only person in history incompetent enough to lose money owning a casino.

Myth-based organizations tend to support tyranny because both the tyrant and the myth-based organization prefer simplistic answers to complex questions and have a shared interest in controlling the lives of ordinary citizens. Tyrants know that myth-based organizations can be useful in the early stages of tyranny and can easily be dispensed with later on. Thus this alliance is a common feature of early-stage tyrannies despite its highly predictable later fracturing.

It is also a sad fact that at all times and in all places, ordinary people have supported repression of minorities. When you're feeling anxious there's nothing as good as being unpleasant to others. It provides a warm glow in the heart and, very often, in the ovens too.

Ordinary decent Germans looked the other way when the Nazis came to round up their Jewish neighbors. But so too did ordinary Americans support the illegal internment of more than 120,000 innocent US citizens of Japanese ethnic origin during World War II. Meanwhile ordinary French and Hungarians and Poles rather eagerly assisted in the detention and deportation of Jews to the Nazi concentration camps, not least because the deportations provided a lot of property for ordinary decent people to appropriate for themselves.

Lest we are tempted to think moral turpitude was confined to the 1930s, US citizens turned a blind eye to illegal bombing of non-combatant nations and the deaths of thousands of innocent civilians during the VietNam war. During the so-called "war on terror" Republican voters strongly approved of government-organized kidnapping and torture. Recently Trump voters strongly supported the Administration's policy of intentional child abuse whereby small children were literally torn from the arms of their parents, placed in cages, and told they would never see their parents again.

These are just a few of the horrors that have happened in democracies, horrors all supported by ordinary decent people who claim to have strong moral values.

So we are for the most part incapable of thinking coherently, are easily gulled by unscrupulous charlatans and thugs, refuse to admit our mistakes, and are happy to be cruel to those whom we've decided are not part of our cozy self-satisfied group. Democracy fails to cope with our hardwired behaviors and our intellectual limitations.

We can see therefore that our system of governance has so many fundamental flaws that it is entirely unsuitable. It's broken and there's no way to fix it. We need to toss representative democracy into the trash-bin of history and begin to fashion something more adequate to meet the very urgent challenges we now face.

Keystone Problems

It is not surprising that as we lurch chaotically towards the end of our accidental experiment with representative democracy, voices should be raised to propose alternatives. Unfortunately most of the strident voices that have so far spoken up offer nothing but the follies of people who willfully ignore those aspects of human behavior that don't fit well with their pet theories.

In the USA we hear clamoring for a "return to natural society" in which people leave one another in peace and trade with each other when such trade is expedient and generally get on with their lives free from government interference. Freedom is secured by means of small arms and stockpiles of ammunition. The fact this idealized "frontier society" has never existed in the history of our species appears to be no impediment to those promoting this particular non-solution.

There are a great many cogent reasons why such a frontier society cannot exist and why less sophisticated societies are in fact more violent, far less productive, and practically never innovative in any way. Such objections are ignored by those promoting their simplistic panaceas because any hint of realism would get in the way of publishing deals and speaking engagements.

An equally egregious notion is that somehow we can paper over the cracks with shiny new technologies. People advocating this approach appear to believe that all citizens are highly intelligent, very well informed about important matters, and can rationally assess and select policies that are designed to ameliorate current problems. Doubtless this view of the world is very comforting to those proposing it; unfortunately real-world data reveals that the typical citizen is the precise opposite of the type assumed by such models. Blockchains, to cite a currently trendy fixation, can no more address the core problems of democracy than a screwdriver can address the core problems of quantum mechanics. Meanwhile artificial intelligence is a much-cited but highly implausible savior, being both an immature technology and highly sensitive to accidental bias.

Not unexpectedly, as democracy's failings become more and more apparent, some old ideas are being dredged up and offered as potential replacements. In Europe the fact that communism, socialism, and nationalism all failed abysmally does not deter the old die-hards for whom ideology matters more than real-world outcomes. After the fiasco of Boris Johnson, formerly Court Jester to the British Conservative Party, the United Kingdom is likely to elect an incompetent lifelong fringe protestor whose only thought is to return the UK to the failures of the early 1970s in which grotesquely inefficient nationalized industries were crippled by trades unions which ensured their members spent more time striking than actually working. The litany of past failure does not deter a new generation of young enthusiasts for they have not read the history books and are thus blithely ignorant of the fact that the supposedly wonderful new ideas of enforced socialist equality are in reality stale old failed nostrums lacking in all validity.

Lastly we see those who believe that dictatorship along the lines favored by Xi Jinping in China is a plausible solution because it appears to offer the promise of long-term planning, social cohesion, and high economic growth. The Soviet Union, however, amply demonstrated the futility of State-controlled long-term planning, social cohesion in China requires increasingly extreme coercion backed by unbridled force, and China's economic growth is inevitably slowing now that it has come some way towards catching up with the level of developed nations. Yet China is ill-prepared to cope with the coming overhang of citizens reaching retirement age while many infrastructure investments are merely money poured down a massive drain.

Today the battle is not really between democracy and less adequate alternatives. Today the battle is between ignorance and facts. Populists everywhere are taking advantage of the gullibility of ordinary people and traditional politicians are either left on the sidelines or are scrambling to jump aboard the nearest populist bandwagon.

At root, populism arises from a deep conviction that we ought to have more: more toys, more food, more power, more security. We have rights! If we want free ice-cream forever, it's our right! Anyone who tries to claim there are valid reasons why we can't have free ice-cream forever is a liar and a traitor and an enemy of the people! Facts are just fake news or part of "project fear" designed to stop us from getting the free ice-cream we deserve.

Clearly *They* are to blame. Who is *They*? They is, well... *Them*. The elites. Politicians. Experts. Some other people. Not *Us*. Because *Us* is good. *Us* wants free ice-cream because, well, we want it. Forever. So we have to protest and shout and make *Them* listen. *They* have grown too powerful and much too big and *They* aren't giving us the free ice-cream that's our inalienable right to consume endlessly without any consequences whatsoever. *They* is also the immigrants who are miraculously simultaneously living off State handouts while assiduously stealing our jobs – especially the jobs we don't want to do. *They* is, in short, any convenient group that can be blamed for our self-inflicted woes by unscrupulous merchants of fear and anger.

We are told that if only we can replace all the incompetent politicians and replace them with someone who really knows what we want and knows how to get things done, all will be well. A strong leader who knows how to get things done. A leader who will lead us back into the past where everything was better, everyone was happier, and even the weather was more agreeable. In other words, populism is simply a return to the wise rule of the monarch, disguised underneath a thin veneer of pretend-democracy that enables cynical autocrats to assume and thereafter retain power.

What we see when we examine popular discontents is a confused melee of disparate resentments. We find xenophobia, racism, envy, fear, and anger. Everyone except us is to blame: immigrants undermining our cultural norms and speaking languages we can't be bothered to learn, elites performing jobs we don't understand while earning more than we do, television experts and pundits who endlessly confuse us with their opinions, and people who don't look or sound like us. Meanwhile journalists and academics dress up this confused tangle of ignorance and present it as reasoned and reasonable rebellion against the status quo because it would be Politically Incorrect to accept it for what it really is: a hopelessly incoherent tide of folly encouraged ever onward by unscrupulous and cynical public figures.

Added to the general melee of follies are particular confusions. In the USA, a fundamental mistake that many soap-box critics have tended to make is to confuse democracy (a system of governance) with government intrusion into what should be private matters (bureaucratic over-reach). Yet a moment's thought shows this conflation to be entirely mistaken.

We know from the examples of totalitarian regimes in China and the former Soviet Union that intrusion of the State into the private domain is even greater under dictatorships than under democracies. The principal difference is that under totalitarian regimes public goods such as health care services, education, and consumer protection are provided in a desultory manner whereas under democracies a much greater effort is made to provide such services because in general they are vote-winning stratagems. Under democratic governments state intrusion is often clumsy, inept, inconsistent and wasteful; but it is not formally intended to keep citizens fearful and under the heel of the regime.

In the USA, as noted earlier, there is a strain of fantasy that pretends we can all go back to a frontier-style way of life because once we adopt the gold standard and have a gun we have all we need. But if we got rid of the State except as a nominal territorial definition, who would provide the roads and the schools and adjudicate quarrels? Who would impose order upon squabbling neighbors and limit the degree of violence that would otherwise erupt? Who would provide clean water and sanitation and the general freedom from robbery that permits such essential infrastructure to be developed and maintained? Who would provide the laws and systems than enable corporations to create and profit from antibiotics, medical equipment, airplanes, automobiles, smartphones, and a hundred-and-one other luxuries we now take for granted. Examples of States that are indeed little more than territorial definitions include Pakistan and Bangladesh, Sudan and Somalia; the quality of an ordinary person's life in such places is neither to be envied nor emulated. When we ask such fantasists about where these essential goods and services would come from, there is only silence in response.

Some people will say, well, clearly *They* have to provide these things. Along with the free ice-cream. And we should get as much as we want, of everything. Including much lower taxes. But we're not sure who *they* are.

The "frontier society" notion that individuals would spontaneously club together to provide large-scale essential services and complex technological products for themselves is at best delusional and at worst an intentional intellectual fraud upon those seeking alternatives to today's state of affairs.

When we look at reality rather than hyperbole it is striking that often the most ardent supporters of Squint Eastward-style rugged individualism turn out to be highly reliant on civilization in general and on government help in particular.

Two examples will suffice to illustrate the general point. Firstly we note that the US survivalist and promoter of rugged self-sufficiency James, (sic) Wesley Rawles depended on government-subsidized health care and the complex infrastructure inherent in our technological civilization for his heart bypass operation and remains reliant on Medicaid for his daily medications. For our second example not so may years ago we enjoyed the highly edifying spectacle of government-subsidized cattle ranchers in the Pacific Northwest protesting against a plan to require them to pay more adequate land use fees; they occupied a government building and proudly proclaimed their independence from all US authorities… until a more heavily armed band of overweight ideologues turned up, at which point the proud tough independent ranchers begged the US authorities to come and save them.

As a side-note we can observe that those who voted for Trump in the 2016 presidential election were disproportionately reliant on government subsidies which they regarded as their "due entitlements" even as they agitated against "the undeserving poor" who in imagination if not in reality were supposedly the main recipients of government largesse. We can also note that despite traditional Republican Party jeremiads against "welfare queens" the US Government Accountability Office (GAO) reported in 2016 that only 3% of welfare payments were potentially fraudulent whereas more than 20% of government payments to large defense and contracting corporations were potentially fraudulent. Yet neither Trump nor the GOP as a whole is willing to mention persistent corporate fraud, never mind take action against it. This is because large corporations (a) make large campaign contributions, and (b) loudly proclaim how many Americans they are employing in key Congressional districts.

We can also note, before moving on, that Trump voters were so astonishingly ignorant that a great many of them voted for the orange buffoon because he promised to repeal Obamacare which was socialist and therefore wrong; but they were very much in favor of the wonderful Affordable Care Act that was provided so many of them with life-saving medications to off-set the health-damaging effects of their obese sedentary junk-consuming lifestyles. The fact that Obamacare *was* the Affordable Care Act was beyond the comprehension of Trump's supporters. Although he is a repellent creature, Trump has done the world the single great favor of demonstrating beyond any doubt whatsoever the true intellectual capacity of a huge percentage of the population.

Remaining with the USA for a while longer, we often find that those clamoring for "less government meddling" are also those seeking much greater intrusion into other people's personal lives. Thus the cry for "smaller government" is accompanied by a cry for laws against a wide variety of personal freedoms ranging from a woman's right to control her reproductive system to denial of equal rights for people based on gender, sexual orientation, and religious belief. When such repressive laws are enacted they not only intrude into the personal realm but also necessarily require an extension of government oversight in order to ensure enforcement.

Have we mentioned that in general we aren't very smart and we almost always fail to understand the implications of our desires?

Returning to the important question of delivery and accepting therefore that we do need some kind of State to provide a rule of law and the provision of critical services, we need now to consider how such things are to be provided. All civilizations since written history began have solved this problem by creating bureaucracies.

Surprisingly, most political commentary has little to say about bureaucracy. People argue endlessly over policy but the issue of policy implementation is at best a minor after-thought. It's as if thinking is sufficient; doing is assumed to occur automatically. But without a bureaucracy of some type, who will implement all those clever new policies that will supposedly make our lives so much better?

Unfortunately we know from experience that bureaucracies can leave a great deal to be desired. Bureaucracies tend to become bloated and ineffectual at best, and at worst they become organizations in which bribery is required in order for anything to get done.

So now we can safely say that the two principal sources of errors inherent in all systems of government are: (A) the formulation and adoption of policy, and (B) the implementation of policy.

There are two main ways today in which policy initiatives arise in democratic nations. The first is directly from special interest groups. In the USA it is typical for lobbyists to draft legislation that is then handed to paid-for politicians who subsequently pretend they originated it in the interests of the citizenry. The second is from politicians themselves who believe that particular misguided policies will appeal to particular voting blocs and therefore increase their chances of continued electoral success.

Only the persistently naïve could imagine that either of these two approaches to policy formulation are likely to result in anything remotely approaching satisfactory outcomes for the nation as a whole.

With policy implementation we see an equally marred landscape. On the one hand a great many civic challenges require long-term solutions but the exigencies of democratic politics within the confines of relatively short election cycles means that short-termism is all that is available. So one inadequate approach cedes place to its equally inadequate successor which in turn cedes place to the next, thus ensuring that none have sufficient time to work, in the unlikely event that one may have been well-formulated enough to withstand even the briefest encounter with reality.

Meanwhile bureaucracies quite naturally tend towards self-preservation so that over time complacent incompetence comes to be regarded as the highest virtue and any impulse towards innovation and greater effectiveness is rapidly quashed.

The cumulative effect is that inept policies are handed over to ineffectual civil servants. Not surprisingly the results are generally not good by any objective measure, unless you happen to make your living from writing satirical television shows.

So we need to do better. A lot better.

Getting Things Done

In the USA it has been common for some years for certain types of politician and agitator to proclaim a desire for "smaller government" as though this could be a solution to contemporary problems of governance. But what do such calls amount to? Merely more spending on the politician's own pet projects and less spending on someone else's. Furthermore, simply reducing the scale of the bureaucracy cannot in and of itself do anything to address the underlying systemic problems inherent in all bureaucratic structures. What do we get if we pair down a bloated ineffectual system? Just a slightly less bloated ineffectual system.

If we want better roads, new schools, and a more adequate electrical grid then we really do need someone to be responsible at the very least for channeling appropriate funds to those with the skills necessary to deliver them. And that means we need some form of bureaucracy. We will shortly look at possible ways to create a reasonably efficient bureaucracy while guarding against the inevitable tendency towards bloat and self-preservation.

We face a dilemma when we think about administration. On the one hand we want to have the most efficient execution of policy initiatives and the most skilled negotiators. This implies a permanent cadre of specialists who over time increase their skills, understanding, and capacities. Yet we know that a permanent cadre of specialists will, over time, come to pursue their own interests at the expense of the population in general.

In some representative democracies, nations have imposed term limits on representatives in an attempt to restrain the inevitable self-serving tendencies we all exhibit. For example, US Presidents are restricted to two four-year terms. We can see the problems that arise when no term limits are present, as is the case with US senators and members of Congress. For these people perpetual campaigning is the norm, which is little more than the perpetual selling of political favors to wealthy donors and groups. Term limits cannot eliminate the pay-to-play problem but they can diminish it a little.

If term limits go some way towards helping minimize the problems of perpetual incumbents, perhaps we can apply the concept of term limits to a cadre of bureaucratic specialists whose purpose is to serve a direct democracy.

There's already a degree of turn-over in our contemporary bureaucracies. Although those who seek careers as bureaucrats tend to be those who prioritize safety, stability, and predictability over other workplace attributes it is nevertheless true that occasionally one or two will leave the bureaucracy to pursue career opportunities elsewhere; and even if no bureaucrat voluntarily retires it is inevitable that eventually retirement or the grave will beckon. So even the most sclerotic bureaucracies must to some degree deal with the requirement for personnel change. Can a bureaucracy be developed to cope with regular personnel changes such as would arise from imposition of (for example) a five-year term limit?

At first there seem to be two major problems with the concept of a restricted-term bureaucracy. The first is that term limits may perversely encourage people to exploit the potential inherent in their position to the maximum degree possible as they know that they only have a short time in which to monetize their power. We see many examples of this across the developing world where bureaucrats and politicians regard their posts as choke-points that enable the extraction of bribes, kick-backs, and other rent-seeking activities. So term limits alone are no guarantee of probity. And if you're a bureaucrat who spends most of your time snatching bribes, chances are you don't really have the time or interest to perform your nominal role with any degree of adequacy. If you doubt this, just hop on a flight to any central African nation.

Secondly, it is obvious that most people hope for financial stability over the course of their working lives. Job changes can be traumatic even when voluntary. Today State bureaucracies recruit directly, and offer jobs for life. If the State can't offer job security, how will it recruit the specialists it needs?

With the exception of certain defense and internal policing actions, any function required of a government bureaucracy is also required within any sufficiently complex commercial organization. The primary difference between commercial organizations and government bureaucracies is that ultimately commercial organizations are answerable to the market. Consequently they must restrict their internal bureaucracies as much as possible while achieving the output necessary for regulatory compliance and operational support. Although individual managers in such internal bureaucracies will inevitably seek to grow the size of their fiefdoms in order to advance their own careers there is far more of a constraint upon bureaucratic bloat than operates in the so-called public sector. Furthermore, management techniques and the overall ethos of efficiency are more highly developed within the commercial sector precisely because efficiency is the ultimate standard by which such groups are measured by the company's executives and shareholders. Thus bureaucrats working within corporations are, overall, somewhat more competent, capable, and efficient than their peers working within government.

So it looks as if we've identified a source of talent that can be tapped for national purposes. As the skills of a corporate bureaucrat are usually of a far higher standard than those of government peers, this means that the "learning curve" to adapt to government service would be small or non-existent. It also means that the latest improvements in processes and technology could more easily be deployed because our temporary bureaucrats would bring with them the knowledge and recent experience of utilizing best practices within a corporate setting.

It is thus not difficult to imagine a process of secondment whereby corporate bureaucrats are appointed to limited-duration government bureaucratic posts. A suitable period would be from two to five years, so that a reasonable balance can be struck between "coming up to speed" and "going native." During the period of secondment individuals would continue to receive, from the government, whatever salaries and benefits were provided by their former employer. Employers would be encouraged, but not obligated, to take back personnel post-secondment. A suitable transition period income guarantee would reduce financial risk for those seconded.

And let's face it: the concept of secondment is already used in modern democracies without any of the ameliorations proposed above. Jurists are required to serve at very little notice upon juries that may sit for up to a year and the recompense they receive is negligible compared to foregone income. Reservist military personnel are likewise deployed for up to a year when the need arises and once again the recompense they receive is small in comparison to personal disruption they experience and the income many are forced to forego. The approach we are proposing is more equitable and it would be an easy matter to give six or even twelve months of advance notice in order to minimize personal disruption. Furthermore, if such secondments were regarded as highly prestigious, personal aversion to temporary disruption would thereby be reduced.

So we may have at least the beginnings of a way to solve the bureaucracy problem.

Next, we can eliminate a lot of the bureaucracy by eliminating the many absurd policies that today create much unnecessary burden on the public and require an army of bureaucrats to administer. As is so often the case, the USA provides the "how not to do things" lesson for the rest of the world. The Internal Revenue Service (IRS) oversees a tax code that contains nearly a century of political manipulation and which is so complex that even the IRS's own specialists get things wrong more than thirty percent of the time. In Florida, if you wish to be employed as a hair stylist, you need twenty-three separate certifications and permits. In far too many States it is illegal to obtain one's electricity or water from anywhere else but the local monopoly utility company. In Oregon a man was jailed for collecting rainwater off his roof, as this violated the requirement for him to obtain all of his water from the assigned regional utility. In Florida a woman was jailed for installing solar panels on her roof and thus reducing the amount of electricity she obtained from her local monopoly utility.

All of these idiocies, and so many more, are the result of politicians creating laws in response to lobbying by special interest groups seeking to gain advantage for themselves, and all these idiocies impose huge hidden costs on society as a whole. By eliminating politicians we eliminate the source of unnecessary regulation, and so our bureaucratic burden shrinks dramatically.

Technology can also reduce the burden of bureaucracy. Countries such as Norway and Estonia have shown that properly designed computer systems can provide many social services. Computer systems can be efficient and unbiased, which are highly desirable traits we don't always find in real-world bureaucracies. So we can reduce the need for a permanent cadre of bureaucrats through thoughtful implementation of service-oriented computer systems provided that these are transparent and can be upgraded as we continue to learn how to improve the delivery of essential services.

As computer systems have no impulse to self-propagate, technology also minimizes the inevitable "bureaucratic bloat" so common to all forms of administration. Although many Western countries have had unhappy experiences with huge IT systems that cost a fortune and fail to deliver promised benefits, countries such as Estonia show that such systems can be developed and implemented effectively when approached in a competent manner.

Lastly, our modern computer and communications technologies mean that for the first time we can demand and obtain a significant degree of transparency. Every decision can be scrutinized, every seconded expert's personal income and other assets can be held up for view, and consequent opportunities for corrupt gains are thus largely eliminated. Norway has led the world in this area and has proven that corruption and incompetence can be significantly reduced by the simple expedient of making data available to anyone who wants to see it.

Nevertheless, even if we automate a majority of services and functions, we'll still be left with an irreducible core of activities that must be performed by humans. Examples include not only the administration of some aspects of public policy but also the staffing of military and law-enforcement organizations as well as public health services. Which means we must address the question: how do we organize a bureaucracy so as to minimize capture and complacency while maximizing competence?

One clear lesson from the study of bureaucracy is that information flows are frequently intentionally restricted in order to provide position power and hence bargaining power to incumbents. This is a variation of the old adage "knowledge is power." In the private sector this includes specialists hoarding proprietary knowledge in order to increase the value of their services; managers hoarding information within their department in order to increase the value of their incumbency; and organizations hoarding knowledge in order to achieve bargaining power over consumers of their products and services. Ironically this hoarding results in systemic inefficiencies that, individually, each organization would normally seek to reduce. For example, all commercial organizations want to reduce unnecessary overheads by becoming more efficient; yet their desire to hoard what they regard as proprietary information means that collectively each organization is far from the efficiency it could attain if all organizations pooled certain categories of knowledge.

What do we mean by this? Let's imagine the following scenario: Organization X wishes to implement a complex computer system in order to automate aspects of its manufacturing, logistics, accounting, and customer service activities. It almost certainly lacks the internal capabilities necessary, so the logical course of action is to outsource the selection and implementation processes to a specialized third party. Unfortunately, however, it will be difficult to select such a specialized third party without having the very skills that are absent within the organization. Without such internal skills and knowledge, how will the organization know which third party is best able to deliver what is required?

By way of analogy, if I don't know how to drive, how can I assess the skills of several different drivers, all of whom are telling me that they are highly skilled and better than their competitors? What criteria can I possibly use that will enable me to have better-than-chance odds of making the optimal selection? In real life, organizations rarely select the optimal choice, opting instead for other characteristics such as price, personal relationships, the desire to avoid censure from above, the illusion of reduced risk, or bribes. This results in a sub-optimal choice of computer system and a sub-optimal implementation, which then damages the overall performance of the organization.

Such sub-optimal choices can be avoided if everyone is sharing information transparently. Instead of the organization being steered towards a select few "customer references" based on the fact that these are the relatively happy customers (we can imagine that few if any organizations actively point potential new customers towards dissatisfied past or present customers...) the organization could avail itself of the collective knowledge base and thereby make a more optimal decision regarding not only the specialist third party but also the computer system itself

This example does not imply that knowledge transparency always results in a perfectly optimal outcome; merely that it will always result in a better outcome than any alternative approach. Throughout this book we are always looking for "better than today's situation" rather than a Panglossian "best of all possible outcomes in this best of all possible worlds."

Transparency of information will also tend to alleviate one of the perennial problems of a bureaucracy: unresponsiveness to consumer needs.

Career bureaucrats are rarely if ever paid on the basis of performance. Instead, bureaucrats trade potential high income for job security and predictability and, usually, generous pension arrangements. This means that they wish to avoid being the subject of complaints because complaints will tend to have an adverse impact on their working conditions such as increased supervisory oversight and potentially a more limited future career path. In order to minimize potential for complaints, bureaucrats will tend to abide strictly to the letter of the law rather than to its spirit; they will also tend to take a longer-than-necessary time to perform their duties in order to minimize throughput which has the effect of minimizing potential complaints. If bureaucrat A processes 50 tasks in a week that creates 50 potential sources of complaint whereas if bureaucrat B processes 5 tasks in a week that creates only 5 potential sources of complaint. In an environment where there is little or no reward for productivity, there is essentially no penalty for a glacial rate of work. From the bureaucrat's perspective, slow is good.

For the rest of us, however, slow is definitely not good. The economic impact of slow bureaucracies can be extensive: delayed planning permission for new roads and buildings, delayed implementation of new policies, delayed hiring of new teachers and police officers, and so on. The total cost to society of the bureaucrat's inertia is literally incalculable but is clearly huge. We want to avoid this outcome when we implement a secondment-based bureaucracy.

When information is transparent to all, a slow work rate is (a) evident, and (b) becomes a poor strategy for minimizing potential complaints. Information transparency serves to "keep people honest" in all directions. It limits the opportunity of consumers to benefit from, as well as suffer from, bureaucratic errors. It limits the ability of bureaucrats to "hide" within their organizations. And it exposes overall efficiency or lack thereof, thus ultimately forcing improvements.

So one aspect of any well-designed bureaucracy (and indeed of any well-designed society) is information transparency. Kleptocrats, dictators, bureaucrats, and ill-intentioned individuals all have a strong incentive to hide information; conversely a free open society has strong incentives to make as much information as possible transparent.

Information transparency, it turns out, plays a hugely important role in self-governance so it is worthwhile to give some additional examples of its efficacy here in order to prepare us for the next part of this book.

Most of us casually assume that secrets are essential. For example, governments keep many details of their military capabilities top secret and they keep secret the precise conditions under which they would act either in aggression or in defense. Indeed, many nations make these decisions on an *ad hoc* basis which dramatically increases uncertainty and therefore risk of miscalculation.

We know from historical evidence that nearly all wars are the result of miscalculation rather than cold deliberation. Each side, having imperfect knowledge of the adversary and often creating policy on-the-fly, tends to over-estimate its chances of success and under-estimate the potential of the adversary to inflict crushing damage. By the time battle has commenced it is too late to reverse the decision to engage in military conflict and so a great many lives will be lost before one or both sides finally tires of the futility and sues for peace.

To see how such transparency enables such miscalculation to be avoided, let's imagine the following scenario: Novia decides on a policy of information transparency while Zemla continues to pursue the traditional approach of secrecy and *ad hoc* decision-making. Novia publishes all information about its weapons systems and its defensive posture (e.g. the circumstances under which it will engage military force in pursuit of its own interests and/or survival). Zemla remains secretive and naturally assumes that Novia's published information is a ruse designed to deceive. At some point Zemla will initiate a "test" of Novia's declared posture. Provided that Novia responds precisely as advertised and that this response is sufficiently robust, Zemla will learn that the published information is correct and therefore an accurate guide to Novia's future actions. Uncertainty and risk is thus reduced even though Zemla has not changed its posture regarding secrecy.

In order for Novia to maintain combat effectiveness, precise battle strategy and tactics must be hidden; however its general posture and capability should be public. Even a nation that has limited defensive capability will be better off publishing its capabilities and intended posture. We can perform the following thought experiment to see why.

Neomonte has a limited military capacity. Its immediate neighbor Rascalia has a large military organization and its leaders are secretive and aggressive and have territorial designs on Neomonte.

If Neomonte keeps the full strength of its capability secret and likewise hides its intentions in the event of aggression, Rascalia will tend to over-estimate its chances of success if it launches a pre-emptive assault on its neighbor; however to reduce the chances of setback Rascalia will tend to maximize the scale of its assault because of its imperfect knowledge regarding its adversary's capabilities and intentions. So Neomonte will suffer greater-than-necessary harm when Rascalia attacks. Equally, if Neomonte defends itself vigorously, Rascalia will suffer greater-than-expected harm even if it is ultimately successful in conquering its neighbor.

Conversely, if Neomonte reveals its full capability and its intentions, one of two outcomes is probable. If Neomonte reveals that in the event of an attack it will not defend itself, Rascalia is likely to launch a probing attack of much lesser magnitude than an all-out assault in order to test the validity of Neomonte's declaration. In this case Neomonte suffers less harm than would be the case with an outright overwhelming assault. Conversely if Neomonte reveals its full capabilities along with a declared intention to inflict as much damage as possible on any adversary attempting to invade it, Rascalia is less likely to miscalculate the outcome of an attack. In the event that Rascalia nevertheless decides to invade, the harm caused to Neomonte will be at most equal to and definitely not be greater than the harm resulting from a state of mutual uncertainty.

And from a tactical perspective, Neomonte's defensive actions are far more likely to be effective because they can be executed immediately without military commanders having to wait for instructions from psychologically unprepared politicians who invariably vacillate in the face of conflict.

So even in the worst-possible scenario the damage to the transparent nation is merely equal to the harm resulting from secrecy and in all other scenarios the outcome will be less harmful either because the aggressor mounts a probing attack rather than an all-out assault or because the aggressor decides that the cost of victory would be too great and therefore refrains from attack altogether.

From this thought experiment we see that it is not necessary for both sides to become transparent in order to reduce the risk of miscalculation; it is sufficient that one side does so unilaterally.

Information transparency is not an all-or-nothing phenomenon. In the example above, Neomonte would reveal its military capabilities and its intentions but would keep its tactical battle plans secret lest precise knowledge of its planned response should permit the aggressor to devise counter-tactics in advance. But there is a huge difference between keeping tactics secret and keeping strategy and capabilities secret. The latter should be transparent while the former should be opaque.

Lest any reader be in doubt about the benefits of transparency in the realm of defense we can cite a real example: the Cold War. During decades of mutual antipathy the Warsaw Pact countries and NATO faced off across the plains of Europe. Although the Warsaw Pact nations did their best to keep their capabilities hidden, NATO regularly exposed its primary capabilities to visiting Soviet representatives during war games. This enabled the Soviets to develop a more accurate assessment of NATO's capabilities and, in private, contrast it with their own capabilities. Although the Warsaw Pact had more troops and more equipment, these troops were poorly trained, unmotivated, and their equipment was sub-standard. Their command-and-control systems were primitive and their overall fighting capacity was limited. No Soviet general believed his battalions would stand up to even modest NATO resistance. NATO meanwhile over-estimated Soviet capability but as NATO never intended to be the aggressor, this was relatively unimportant. It can be argued, therefore, that transparency on the part of NATO was a major reason why the Cold War never turned hot: USSR military and intelligence personnel had a reasonably accurate assessment of NATO capability. Transparency is a good thing.

The Need for Speed

The next question we need to address is a more challenging one: how shall we assign responsibility for activities that are not suitable for direct decision-making yet are not well suited to action through a bureaucracy? These will most often be when exogenous challenges require a rapid and coherent response.

Examples of such problem classes include:

- Responding to external aggression (covert or overt) by another nation or by non-State actors

- Negotiating treaties (for example, treaties on trade, on climate change mitigation, on international rules such as the Law of the Sea, and on mutual-assistance) with other nations where such negotiations often require rapid adjustments to initial policy positions

- Deciding on appropriate action to deal with atypical issues such as providing aid after a natural disaster

In representative democracies these decisions are taken by the Executive branch of government but in a direct democracy there will be no Executive branch. Yet it is infeasible to imagine even the most informed and always-on society being able to respond collectively to exogenous requirements and shocks quickly and coherently enough.

At all times in history, even when direct democracy was in effect (as in ancient Athens, for example) societies have chosen to appoint leaders in order to ensure rapid and effective centralized decision-making and task execution. The question for us today is: can we imagine an alternative that is better than handing considerable power into the hands of an individual or small group of individuals? Because when significant power is handed over, "temporarily" tends to become "permanently." The world is littered today with "democracies" that are in reality nothing other than decades-long rule by strongmen and their henchmen.

We need a solution that enables the necessary speed and effectiveness of executive action without the attendant risks of self-aggrandizement, group-think, or inadequate comprehension of the situation. Nor must personality exert undue influence on outcomes. World War Two occurred largely because Hitler was able to assess Chamberlain and Daladier and determine that they (like the citizens who had elected them) were terrified of conflict and would do practically anything in order to try to avoid it. Knowing how psychologically weak his opponents were gave Hitler the confidence to press forward with his territorial expansion.

One of the many failings of representative democracy is that it puts into the hands of the Executive the responsibility for making decisions of national importance. Top politicians succeed because they've put themselves first and the needs of the nation second. Their decisions are perpetually influenced by political considerations. They are accustomed to using empty words to achieve their aims and generally build entire careers on a careful avoidance of consequences. After a long period of peace, no European politician is capable of more than squabbling over the precise choice of empty words to be used in a meaningless communique. So when life produces real challenges, most "leaders" do wonderful impersonations of jelly. We saw Europe in full-on jelly mode when in 2014 Russia invaded Ukraine. Western leaders, accustomed to long rounds of bureaucratic negotiations over minute technical details in which the most difficult problem they face is what choice of wine to consume with dinner, were completely incapable of grasping what Putin had done and equally incapable of formulating any meaningful response.

Even more revealing was the failure of Western leaders to respond appropriately to the election of Trump to the White House. This left many of the world's leaders utterly unable to comprehend and formulate effective strategies for dealing with the reality of an infantile halfwit occupying the world's most powerful office. Germany's Angela Merkel attempted to use reason while France's young President Emmanuel Macron attempted to use charm and flattery. Both strategies failed abysmally because both were based on a total failure to recognize Trump's extreme cognitive limitations. If Western leaders are incapable of dealing with such a relatively obvious challenge it is clear they are unfit to cope with more onerous duties.

While Marxist theory alleges that grand historical forces shape all outcomes and that individuals are mere bit-players who can be substituted largely without impact, real-world historical analysis demonstrates that on the contrary individuals frequently assume huge importance and dramatically influence the outcome of events. Sometimes a single person can alter the course of history. As the British perpetually claim to have "won" the Second World War, it's worthwhile to examine how the British ended up switching from eager appeasement to reluctant confrontation.

After the total failure of Chamberlain's policy of appeasing Hitler, the King met with the two individuals judged most suitable to lead a government: Halifax and Churchill. The former was a Party grandee and most people's choice; the latter was a known eccentric, something of an outsider and distrusted because of his earlier change of political affiliation. In fact Churchill was only present because he'd consistently warned against the Nazi menace years before anyone was ready to listen. No one expected him to become Prime Minister but it would have been bad form not to have pretended to have considered him.

Protocol indicated that when the King asked who should lead the next government, the junior attendee (Churchill) should cede to the senior (Halifax). Had this happened, Halifax would have become Prime Minister of the UK and would have negotiated a peace treaty with Hitler, leaving the German dictator to enjoy unchallenged hegemony over Europe. Instead, Churchill obdurately remained silent until Halifax, in a classic display of English manners triumphing over self-confidence, ceded place to Churchill. The latter went on to lead the British into the depths of war which at the time was not at all a popular decision.

Had a referendum been called, it is very likely that the majority of British citizens would have voted for more appeasement. In the event however grand "historical forces" meant little in comparison to the determination of one man to push a nation down a different path. It's also worth noting that Churchill utterly ignored "the will of the people" because he knew "the people" was wrong-headed. So, ironically, Western historians were later able to claim that "democracy triumphed over tyranny" only because Churchill ignored the precepts of democracy.

Lest the naïve and romantically-inclined should turn to thoughts of revolution, as was transiently popular with the pampered youth of the 1960s and early 1970s, we must note that revolutions turn out to be even worse than the mistakes of democracy. Every revolution, with the honorable exception of the thirteen colonies of North America breaking away from Britain, tends to result in thugs and psychopaths assuming power because these people feel little or no compunction about sacrificing others in order to advance their own careers. When traditional constraints and rule of law breaks down it is the most ruthless chancers who claw their way to the top. But once in power the character of the individual then plays a significant role. Would so many Ukrainians have died if some person other than Stalin had taken control of the Soviet Party after the death of Lenin? And if Stalin had not died and ceded place to Khrushchev, the Cuban missile crisis could very easily have ended in global thermonuclear war instead of a face-saving climb-down orchestrated largely by the Soviet premier.

Equally, if Mao had not squatted malignantly at the top of the Chinese communist system, would sixty million Chinese have been consigned to death by starvation in consequence of his farcical Great Leap Forward? And if George W Bush had not been in the White House during the September 11th attacks, would the USA have gone on to invade Iraq, which was a nation that had absolutely nothing whatsoever to do with the event that brought down the Twin Towers but instead was a country whose leader represented "unfinished business" for the Bush family?

It is evident therefore that we can turn neither to revolution nor to retaining the status quo if we wish to find better ways to manage ourselves.

It's obvious that any system of governance that wants to be fit for purpose can't put significant power into the hands of any individual person or group for eventually that power will be sorely misused. Yet unless certain kinds of power are (at least temporarily) concentrated, how will urgent exogenous challenges be met?

To see how we can answer this question it is helpful to begin to break down the problem into pieces.

One of the main reasons we assume that exogenous challenges require a centralized executive is because to date societies have done a very poor job of defining their core values. Each political Party takes it in turn to try to sell itself to the electorate and then if it is successful at the ballot box it attempts to impose some of its values through policies that may or may not actually yield some of the desired outcomes. This is akin to letting very small children try to organize and prepare their own school lunches based on nothing more than the transient whims of those too young and inexperienced to make adequate nutritional choices and then select appropriate ingredients and preparation techniques that they can transform into edible results. We all know what happens when we let a group of infants loose on bread dough; the same result is generally true of letting politicians loose with policy initiatives. The only difference is that while children may ruefully acknowledge their output is nothing more than a slimy gooey mess, politicians generally claim success and move on to new "initiatives" that are "guaranteed" to deliver the promised benefits next time.

If we're willing to learn from experience rather than from assertion, many exogenous challenges turn out to be addressable through forethought and the provision of constitutional directives, which reduce the requirement for rapid decision-making in times of crisis.

In practical terms what does this mean? To find out, let's look again at the most extreme situation we are likely to encounter: one country is threatened with military aggression by its neighbor. Although in Europe nearly eighty years of peace have blunted people's perceptions regarding the likelihood of conflict, those living in eastern Europe are necessarily more intimately acquainted with the idea, as any Ukrainian citizen can readily attest.

As we noted earlier, most military adventurism is often a consequence of inadequate information and of each side having an overly-inflated sense of its own ability to achieve a satisfactory outcome. If a nation is transparent regarding its military capability and if the constitution of that nation mandates that any aggression against it will be met with total resistance and if that mandate is supported by sufficient capacity to inflict significant damage on any adversary and if, when tested, the nation responds as advertised, other nations (even those led by mentally inadequate demagogues) will tend to refrain from direct military aggression. Other forms of aggression may be attempted but provided this also triggers a total response, these too will not be attempted again.

By hardwiring a response into the "national system" we can be reasonably confident that potential aggressors will ultimately choose to target other potential victims rather than incur a known significant cost by targeting the nation that has defined its response and proven the value of its words when tested. While a military organization is required to provide the response, no executive body is required to weigh up the usual alternatives such as "let's pretend it's not happening," vacillate, capitulate, authorize a half-hearted reaction, or authorize a forceful reaction too late. Under conditions of total transparency the nation's response is both more coherent and much faster. The value of a surprise attack is thus radically diminished and its probability concomitantly reduced.

To put it in simple terms, a mugger will choose a victim who looks unlikely to fight back. Few muggers, even those whose mental state is disrupted by narcotics, select potential victims who seem ready and able to inflict serious harm on the mugger himself. Nations are, sadly, little different from individuals: small nations may bluster and threaten but none will risk a direct attack on a much stronger adversary. Conversely strong nations feel no inhibition with regard to bullying and invading weaker nations, especially when those weaker nations are led by people whose capacity for dealing with urgent exogenous threats is negligible.

On a smaller scale history shows us that even non-State actors are reliably deterred by evidence of resistance. After the Special Air Service on 5th May 1980 assaulted the Iranian Embassy in London to free the hostages and kill the terrorists, no terrorist group targeted the UK mainland. After ships began to station armed guards who were free to shoot at pirates, the incidence of piracy off the coast of Somalia dropped precipitously. While many comfortable people living safe lives in developed nations may deplore the idea of violence being a solution to some types of problem the fact is that sometimes violence – or the credible threat of violence – is indeed the only answer because aggressors rarely change their minds as a result of lectures on the futility of the use of force. And thus we must hardwire this fact into our systems of government if we wish to avoid becoming prey to those ready and eager to use force to promote their objectives.

Touching on military matters prompts the question: how would a direct democracy avoid the peril of a military coup? History, after all, has no shortage of examples of military men taking power and holding on to it for considerable periods of time.

While it is true that any internal concentration of power, especially of military power, can represent a threat to the stability of a society it is also true that military intrusion into the political realm almost always occurs in response to social disorder. When the political elite is corrupt, venal, incompetent, and ineffectual there is among military men the desire to restore order. Very few coups begin because of ambition alone; while it is obviously self-serving for a Colonel or a General to claim that he is taking power "for the good of the nation" it is also a fact that a great many individuals who do seize power in this way genuinely do so because they believe they have no alternative or because the power vacuum has become so obvious that it is a matter of simplicity to fill it. Very frequently a military takeover of political affairs is greeted enthusiastically by a public grown weary of the endless scandals plaguing the clique of corrupt, ineffectual, and squabbling professional politicians.

If a direct democracy can tend to its affairs with at least as much probity and competence as a typical civilian administration (and we are mindful of the fact that this is not exactly a very demanding threshold) then there is little excuse for a military coup to occur. In fact the very absence of a distinct political class renders almost void the psychological conditions necessary for such an event, just as the norms of democratic governance in the West render such coups unlikely despite the evident dissatisfaction people have with their political representatives. It is not the presence of politicians who prevent coups and it is not their absence that makes coups more likely. Indeed the causal relationship is precisely the opposite: without a professional political class, coups become less likely provided civil society continues to function adequately.

The only time a coup may become possible is if a charismatic rabble-rouser should emerge and appeal to the less enfranchised and to the entirely disenfranchised, claiming to represent their interests and seeking to seize power and return the nation to some form of dictatorship. In this event, however, it is more plausible to imagine the civil powers such as the police acting to restrain a return to mob rule than to imagine the military seeing an opportunity to impose themselves upon the nation. Nevertheless, any concentration of power and force must be carefully managed and once again full transparency is essential to social stability.

It is also clear that any stable society requires both an educational system that encourages individuals to acquire facts and exercise basic reasoning skills, and an information propagation policy that deters the creation and spreading of falsehoods and rabble-rousing emotional appeals that would undermine society. We shall return to these two criteria later in this book.

The greatest single impediment to a military coup is simply the fact that military personnel are woefully ill-equipped to run a modern complex economy. There is no shortage of examples of ruinous outcomes when generals or colonels or sergeants take charge; conversely there are precisely no examples of persistently successful outcomes. If direct democracy delivers adequate governance it's difficult to imagine how any military regime could hold power for longer than a few years before the great mass of people notice how poorly the nation is performing.

It's apparent that the same thought experiment must likewise be applied to the security services, for they too constitute a powerful "inner organization" that could potentially seize power, albeit with far more difficulty than the military would experience. Again we can note that secret service officers lack the expertise to run a country. Over the last fifteen years Russia has done the world a great service by demonstrating this fact unambiguously.

Turning now to such matters as treaty negotiations with other nations we can see that many of the problems we experience with representative democracy result from economic illiteracy and a resulting confusion about desirable goals. When basic economic principles are built into the Constitution of a nation, many apparently difficult problems can be somewhat mitigated. And although the discipline of economics is still woefully immature and far too reliant on a spreadsheet version of witchcraft, it may ultimately develop into a more adequate intellectual framework by means of which to explore options and encourage better outcomes. Even allowing for the immaturity of economics today, it has provided a few genuine insights which ought to be, but sadly are more often not, utilized to develop national policies. Trade is an important example.

Although innumerate politicians and an even more innumerate population frequently fail to grasp the core concepts of trade, the fact is trade is generally beneficial. While it is true that trade invariably puts some jobs at risk or eliminates them entirely, it benefits society as a whole and creates far more jobs than it destroys. While this is little consolation to those whose jobs are lost, it is untenable to propose that society should in effect subsidize a few unsustainable jobs at the cost of preventing a great many more coming into existence. We can imagine what would have been the fate of a nation that resolutely opposed the invention of the seed drill and insisted that only hand-scattered seeds should be permitted in order to "save" agricultural jobs while all the other nations of the world proceeded to reap the benefits of dramatically higher crop yields.

A Constitution that enshrines the fundamental precepts of trade could avoid the endless political posturing common in today's democratic societies and preclude the foolish self-harming policies that result from politicians seeking to pander to a tiny minority who wish to retain their jobs at the expense of society as a whole. It has been very common in democracies for those whose jobs may be threatened to make emotional appeals designed to "save" their occupations at the cost to everyone else. For example fishermen, having depleted fish stocks by years of over-fishing, will appear on television lamenting the loss of their livelihoods. As the media has a perpetual appetite for stories that have emotional resonance, such lamentations will receive wide coverage. Sympathy is elicited and subsidies are granted.

But who pays for these subsidies? The general population, and the global environment. Fishermen continue to over-fish, exterminating fish stocks and thus increasing the price of fish. Likewise coal miners, workers in steel mills, automobile workers, and a nearly endless list of others have all at various times imposed upon their societies to "save" jobs by imposing goods on society as a whole at a greater price than those goods should have commanded. It is a successful strategy because the average citizen is entirely unable to grasp the simple mechanics of the transaction and thus the public collaborates in cheating itself.

The only circumstance in which trade does genuinely present deep jeopardy is when one nation seeks to use trade primarily as a strategic weapon against others. Modern examples include Russia's desire to make much of Europe dependent on its natural gas, and China's desire to lock developing nations into debt in return for modest Chinese-delivered infrastructure improvements. Whereas representative democracies are highly vulnerable to such ploys because citizens are largely ignorant of the consequences and politicians are eager for the short-term benefits they can tout in order to gain re-election, a more adequately governed nation should seek to make more adequate decisions based on an informed and coherent appraisal of overall risks and benefits.

Trade can also be immensely stupid even when no one is attempting to use trade in a strategic way. For example, the West has for decades been selling sophisticated weaponry to pretty much any nation with the cash required, yet these nations then go on to create regional instability that costs much Western treasure to attempt to mitigate. Even worse, it's not unknown for Western armies to end up being bombed and shot at by the very weapon systems produced by their own countries. The short-term quest for profit generally outweighs any medium to long term rationale; no executive can for long veto such "job creating" sales. So we must do better when we replace representative democracy with something more fit for purpose.

Regarding multinational negotiations on such things as food standards, cross-border energy coordination, mutual defense treaties and the rest, it is not difficult to imagine qualified citizens proposing and voting upon appropriate policy positions and then passing these to a cadre of seconded bureaucrats to ensure implementation. And because these national policies would be transparent and based as much as possible on what is best for the country rather than what is most politically expedient, the other nations around the table would have much less room to attempt to enforce the distortions typical of international treaties and agreements. It's difficult to horse-trade when the other side has given up horses.

While nations still laboring under representative democracies and those suffering under tyranny would continue to experience all the harms engendered by their systems of governance, the fact that one player at the table was unresponsive to such antics would inevitably reduce the degree of game-playing possible which in turn would ultimately benefit everyone concerned. Over time other nations too might come to regard their political systems as unfit for purpose and likewise begin to experiment with direct qualified democracy, thus improving outcomes more widely.

As the reader thinks through other examples of the areas in which executive action is typically required in representative democracies, it will become apparent that in a great many cases the need for a failure-prone Executive can be eliminated through the constitutional provision of coherent policies based on real-world data aimed at producing the best possible outcome under the widest possible range of circumstances. We therefore don't really need an Executive for most exogenous challenges. Most necessary negotiations can be left to temporary teams of technocrats operating under strict guidelines and whose fruits can then be put to the ballot so qualified voters can indicate acceptance or rejection.

Competence is Good

Now that we've sketched some possible solutions to the problem of policy implementation we need to move on to the larger question of policy creation.

Today we automatically assume that policy and Party are nearly synonymous. Parties develop policies they believe will be popular with the electorate, and the electorate votes for policies it thinks will benefit them. In reality however many policies are specious and impossible to implement and many are merely window-dressing for rules that actually favor the wealthy and powerful. Even more damaging is the fact that because so many of us are quite simple-minded we often vote not for the policy but for the person promoting it. These days that usually means the most entertaining performer. Boris Johnson in the UK is a demonstrably egregious and incompetent person but because he was amusing he secured high office and helped wreck the future of the United Kingdom by promoting a policy (Brexit) he knew to be illusory yet which he thought could aid his personal ascent to 10 Downing Street. And to be fair to the former Court Jester of the British Conservative Party, his buffoonery had up to that point proven to be a highly successful tactic because people love being entertained. It is so much easier to laugh than to think.

It's clear that as we're generally quite hopeless judges of plausibility, rarely or never perform the intellectual work required to analyze policy for feasibility and outcomes, and are readily swayed by blustering entertainers instead of making rational decisions, we can't assume that we should expect automatically to have any rights with regards to formulation of policy and with regards to voting for (or against) policy.

An alien visiting Earth for the first time would be astonished at the way we handle responsibilities. We require some level of demonstrated competence for almost every aspect of daily life except for two incredibly important things: voting, and having children. While it is beyond the scope of this book (and beyond the author's desire for additional post-publication conflict) to discuss the matter of propagating one's genes, it's obvious that we need a serious re-think of our approach to voting.

We can begin by disposing of so-called representatives. We no longer need anyone to bridge "the tyranny of distance" on our behalf because modern communications technologies permit us to interact instantly with anyone else, anywhere else, at any time of the day or night. We can watch live news feeds rather than learning of events hours, days, or even weeks after they occur. And we can access a wide array of information sources by means of which to obtain a more adequate context than any single source would be likely to provide. So the notion of sending "representatives" to a central debating chamber far away is today entirely anachronistic and redundant. It's time we caught up with the possibilities we've created for ourselves by means of modern communications technologies. We no longer expect to commute to work via a horse-drawn carriage; why should we expect to continue utilizing a form of government that arose back when horse-drawn carriages were the epitome of transportation?

Furthermore, if we toss the concept of representatives into the trash bin of history there will be no obvious targets for the wealthy and the powerful to bribe, suborn, or simply purchase outright. And without representatives, individual citizens won't be able to focus on personality. No longer will it be possible for an entertaining buffoon or a blustering halfwit to secure votes merely because they are memorable. At a stroke a great many of our problems disappear.

With the end of representatives comes the end of political Parties. This in turn means the end of "affiliation voting." In the UK for many years it was typical to hear a voter say, "My father voted Labour and I've voted Labour all my life and I'm not going to change now." In the USA in 2016 many Republicans voted for a repellent orange moron because they were unable to prevent themselves voting for anyone at all who had an "R" next to their name. Such voters would doubtless have endorsed Mussolini or Stalin had these exemplars of liberty possessed the foresight to have claimed affiliation with the US Republican Party. Polity is far too important to be treated as merely equivalent to one's affiliation with a sporting team.

When we've dispensed with representatives we're left with anonymously proposed policies that can only be judged on their merit, not as per today confused with the personality of the politician attempting to sell them to us.

It would be wonderful if every citizen was informed and thoughtful so that policy proposals could be evaluated rationally and voted upon accordingly. As we'll never live in such an ideal world, we need to adjust our expectations. We can start by recognizing that enfranchisement is a privilege that should be earned, not a right to be squandered or abused.

A great many studies have demonstrated beyond all doubt that we humans are largely incapable of voting in a rational manner. For example someone who's recently lost a spouse or partner will tend to vote against the incumbent regardless of economic conditions, policy proposals, or even personality. Likewise more people vote against the incumbent when it is raining and more vote for the incumbent if their sports team has just won a game. There is, sadly, no shortage of evidence that we humans are woefully ill-suited to the business of behaving rationally. Even before the blandishments and simple-minded lies of blustering charlatans we can be relied on to vote foolishly and thus create enormous damage for ourselves and all those around us.

In order to minimize the harmful effects of what can be termed "foolish votes" we must require some qualifications from those seeking to be enfranchised. Just as with any formal education or activity there are degrees of qualification. We don't expect eight-year-olds to display the knowledge and reason we expect of post-graduate students so we tier academic examinations based on age and duration of study. We likewise tier our professions, commencing from the simplest tasks and proceeding by stages to the most complex and demanding. At each point of progression we expect candidates to demonstrate their competence, after which greater responsibility and authority is conferred upon them. The same is true of non-intellectual pursuits such as martial arts. Only a dreamer expects to be granted a black belt on Day One and we don't allow beginners to teach others or open their own schools just because they believe, despite all evidence to the contrary, they'll "make karate great again"

We've also got to set aside Political Correctness and accept the obvious fact that people are not equal. Some are taller, some are more gifted at abstract reasoning, some are more musical, and so forth. We tend when possible to pursue careers for which we have some natural aptitude. Furthermore we know that natural aptitude is not an all-or-nothing quantity. People have varying degrees of talent and determination. We have cellists who play only at home for their own entertainment, we have cellists who play in local amateur orchestras, we have cellists who play in professional orchestras, and we have a very small number of star soloist cellists who travel the world to give performances and masterclasses.

To employ another analogy we can consider aircraft pilots. A relatively unskilled general aviation (private aircraft) pilot must pass the Visual Flight Rules (VFR) test in order to be permitted to fly solo and carry non-paying passengers. In addition there are other restrictions associated with weather and overfly. If the pilot wishes to have a greater range of freedom then it is necessary to pass a more stringent exam and qualify as an Instrument Flight Rules (IFR) certified pilot. After this, pilots wishing to fly more advanced aircraft and have an even wider range of freedoms must qualify appropriately. And when a pilot wishes to fly professionally in either a military or a commercial capacity there are very stringent requirements indeed.

Let's be honest here: we wouldn't want the pilot of our next commercial flight to be in the left seat merely because they felt they deserved it and were convinced that somehow they'd know what to do when the time came and had moreover convinced a suitable number of random members of the public that they would be "the best pilot, the greatest pilot." In fact, we'd be right to storm the cockpit and remove the pilot under such circumstances.

There's plenty of empirical evidence to show that the less a person knows about a topic, the more confident they are that they'd be very skilled at it. This common self-delusion is called the Dunning-Kruger effect, named after the two researchers who first studied it. As there are no formal qualifications required for a career in politics it is not surprising that the Dunning-Kruger effect is widely seen in the political realm and the results are always catastrophic.

In most aspects of life, instead of letting incompetents do whatever they want, we rightly expect the most difficult and important tasks to be assigned to those who have undertaken the effort required to prepare themselves to discharge their responsibilities adequately. We urgently need to apply this basic principle to the world of governance.

If someone isn't interested in becoming sufficiently educated about a particular subject domain, there's no reason for us to grant that person the right to vote in an ignorant and foolish manner and thus degrade the quality of governance, because everyone suffers from ignorant and foolish voting. It is not "fair" to let people vote when they are unqualified to do so; it is in fact manifestly unfair on everyone else.

This all leads us to some conclusions. The first is that it makes sense to employ tiered structures of enfranchisement. The second is that we should require evidence of capability in order to grant enfranchisement at the appropriate level and for the appropriate subject domains.

Unlike the occupational examples cited above, when it comes to government we must also consider how to protect the interests of those who will not achieve substantial enfranchisement. Pilots can't easily discriminate against non-pilots and surgeons can't easily discriminate against non-surgeons but the enfranchised can, by promoting policies that are self-serving, discriminate against the non-enfranchised.

As we humans are self-serving creatures it's implausible to suggest *pace* Plato that an "enlightened autocrat" will be an adequate guardian of the less enfranchised. This is because it is beyond the bounds of human nature for an "enlightened elite" to exist. One or two individuals may make a sincere and prolonged effort to live up to such ideals but the vast majority of us will quickly take advantage of any situation in which we enjoy disproportionate power and influence. We'll return to this issue once we've fully explored the idea of qualified voting.

If we're going to require cognitive capability and domain knowledge as the key determinants of enfranchisement we must ask: is there any reason that enfranchisement should be all or nothing? Just as in our working lives we tend to become specialists and not equally competent in all fields of human endeavor, so it's highly likely that most potential voters will become knowledgeable in one primary domain. For example, Jane may have a great interest in and spend considerable time acquiring information about the economics of international trade but know little about health care policy or national defense. It's entirely appropriate that she should be entitled to vote on matters of international trade but not on matters about which she is largely ignorant.

We also need to understand that knowledge and cognitive capacity are not the same.

Cognitive capacity can be defined as a person's ability to understand fundamental concepts, solve domain problems, and display the ability to follow causal chains. This is different from domain expertise because it's entirely possible for someone to memorize all the arcane details of a particular subject yet be entirely unable to draw logical conclusions from this knowledge or to suggest ways in which things may be improved. Equally, a person could be very clever indeed but have inadequate knowledge of a particular domain which in turn would lead them into error when it comes to matters of policy.

There are, sadly, a great many examples of poor policy being formulated by clever people who lack the necessary domain knowledge. We can cite just one for the sake of illustration: congestion pricing. Today many cities become clogged with traffic during rush hour. Many economists believe that because consumer goods have a certain price-elasticity function the general rule applies to other areas of life as well. In other words, increase the price of something and demand for it will fall. Sounds reasonable, no?

But congestion is not caused by people voluntarily choosing to go to work all at the same time. Here's what actually happens in the real world (a place not often visited by economists): schools demand that children arrive at a set time; companies demand that workers arrive at a centrally-located office at a set time. The result: millions of cars on the roads at the same time of day heading to the same few destinations. No driver has the choice to travel at a different time, regardless of any congestion charge that may be levied for travel at peak hours. No parent wishes to have their child expelled from school because they arrived later than the school's mandated hours of attendance. No worker wishes to lose their job because they commuted to work one hour after peak traffic in order to avoid paying a congestion charge. All a congestion charge does is to levy another tax on those least able to afford it. We can note that the wealthy will rarely if ever pay the charge because wealth enables one to order one's life for convenience rather than necessity.

An intelligent approach to reducing the hours wasted as a result of traffic congestion would recognize the prime drivers of congestion and seek to influence them. Schools are unnecessary in a world in which online learning is readily available and far more effective than classroom-bound education. Companies can be incentivized by means of tax credits and tax penalties to abolish the office altogether and encourage working from home. These approaches would yield superior outcomes for both individuals and society as a whole. But they are never discussed by economists because economists lack the requisite domain expertise, operating as they do entirely in an academic environment far from the realities of everyday life.

Thus we need to combine cognitive capacity with domain expertise. The good news is that we already do this every day: educational establishments test students in precisely this manner, as do vocational bodies. We simply have to apply the same approach to the matter of enfranchisement.

Through proper assessment we can arrive at a reasonable measure of a person's competence in a given domain. It's essential that assessments should not become tests of orthodoxy but instead tests of reasoning, for it is quite valid for someone to reject the current orthodoxy of a particular intellectual domain precisely because they understand it very well. This is, after all, how much scientific progress is made.

And let's be honest: it's obvious that even imperfect early attempts will provide a far better fit between ability and responsibility than today's crude age-based separation between no enfranchisement whatsoever and total enfranchisement thereafter. And over time we can improve our testing methodologies whereas an age-based criterion will always remain utterly inadequate.

There's no necessary limit to the areas of domain expertise any individual can aspire to master. Some people will have a greater interest in learning than others and some may have more leisure time by means of which to acquire knowledge. Likewise some people may find certain domains easier to master than others. But a sufficiently motivated person of appropriate intelligence could achieve enfranchisement to propose and vote upon policies across a wide range of domains.

Some readers who are still emotionally attached to the idea that democracy is not entirely unfit for purpose may ask, "How could a system of government based only on qualified individuals have any legitimacy? Most people would be enfranchised either not at all or only in a very limited way. How could this be fair?"

When we consider the proposition we see that it's empty. Do we say that surgery has no legitimacy because not everyone is a qualified surgeon? Do we claim that air transportation has no legitimacy because not everyone has passed their civil transportation pilot certification? Do we claim the police force has no legitimacy because we don't vote for individual police officers?

Turning things around, we can more reasonably ask: what possible legitimacy can there be for a system that permits huge numbers of people to vote for catastrophically inept politicians and equally inept policies out of a position of near-total ignorance and thoughtlessness? Would we regard our health care system as "legitimate" because it permitted anyone to wander in off the street and perform surgery on the grounds that as a citizen they have a perfect right to do so?

All around us, in nearly every aspect of our lives, we have adopted requirements that must be met before people are permitted to perform specified tasks. We know what happens when a nation doesn't insist on people passing a driving test before being allowed on the road: mass carnage. We can imagine what would occur if we let absolutely anyone over the age of eighteen pilot commercial aircraft merely because they were past the age of majority.

So the objection that a system in which individuals must demonstrate competence before being allowed to propose and vote on policy is somehow "illegitimate" is clearly misguided and no more rational than systems that have claimed an individual should own a certain amount of property in order to be permitted to vote, or should be male rather than female, or must be pale-skinned rather than dark-skinned. And as the dire state of our world indicates, we are long past the point where we can afford to continue to act irrationally.

To be succinct: today we permit people to vote more or less on a whim, unencumbered by understanding or knowledge. This results in the election of people who are ill-suited to the task of governance and whose "policies" are rarely adequate. A more careful matching of capabilities to responsibilities is unlikely to produce worse results than our present nonsensical approach and is far more likely to produce far better outcomes howsoever we choose to define the word "better." The only reason this type of approach will be rejected is because people have come to believe they have a "right" to vote, and will fight hard to retain that right even if they never bother to use it. But just because people will resist change doesn't mean change is wrong. We used to accept people smoking everywhere; now smoking is restricted to certain locations. We used to accept people thrashing small children; now such actions are considered to be criminal offenses. We used to think blood-letting cured disease; now we know it just makes things worse.

The list of improvements we've resisted in the past is very long indeed, so we can conclude that just because we don't want to change something this doesn't mean it shouldn't in fact be changed.

And looking around the world as we've made it today, it is clear that change is desperately needed.

No More Roulette

If we accept it's reasonable to have an explicit relationship between rights and responsibilities in the important matter of governance, we can now look at how individuals may earn the right to vote at different levels and for particular domains of expertise. Instead of our current system, which resembles a kind of roulette where people vote with the same degree of thought as they'd play the wheel in a casino, we can seek to develop a more coherent and facts-based approach to governing ourselves. And to escape from the roulette wheel we need to design something where the odds aren't always with the house – which in the case of representative democracy means the coterie of professional politicians and the special interests that influence them. Instead of running a casino, we need to ensure that rights and responsibilities are given to those who expend the effort necessary to earn them. We already do this in most aspects of our lives; it's long past time we applied the same basic logic to the issue of governance.

To earn enfranchisement in a particular domain and at a particular level (town, region, nation) we should need to undertake a formal test of (a) our reasoning abilities, and (b) our domain knowledge. If our reasoning is faulty and our knowledge is sparse, we clearly aren't ready for the responsibility of voting within that subject domain, never mind voting in a more general way.

In order for us to remain enfranchised at a particular level, we should need to make suitable efforts to remain knowledgeable about those domains in which we wish to exercise our voting rights. Regular re-testing, perhaps every five years or so, would ensure that citizens cannot continue to vote regardless of cognitive decline and ignorance of new information.

It will be essential to ensure that any system of accreditation is developed and overseen as impartially and transparently as possible. Otherwise we'll end up with versions of "Jim Crow" laws designed to preclude particular groups of people obtaining the right to vote. One of the key elements of any system of graduated enfranchisement must be total transparency, for intentional distortions and manipulations are made much more difficult when everyone can examine both contents and outcomes and look for improbable patterns that are indicative of systemic perversion. Equally clearly we need a system of law that can redress any distortions and attempt to preclude similar distortions in future.

Assuming the practical difficulties can be overcome as we learn from experience how better to structure and implement such processes, we can develop multiple tiers of enfranchisement. Not only tiered in the sense of greater domain knowledge but also tiered geographically.

For example, enfranchisement may commence at the smallest collective such as towns, cities, and counties and expand in gradations up to the nation itself. A voter may be perfectly qualified to vote on economic matters at the level of their town but not yet qualified to vote on economic matters at the level of the country as a whole.

This means expertise and locale are comingled; thus Alice may be qualified to vote on a wide range general matters for her city and further qualified to vote only on matters of economic policy for the country as a whole.

Now we need to examine what it means to formulate policy and in addition how positive feedback loops can be constructed so that we can collectively learn from our mistakes and improve our ability to make better decisions in future (a feature which is everywhere notably lacking in our present systems of governance).

What does it mean to formulate public policy? In principle it should include the following steps:

- Statement of current situation

- Problems arising from current situation

- Desired future outcome

- Proposal(s) whereby to increase the probability of the desired future outcome being achieved

- Cost benefit analysis of proposal(s)

- Analysis of potential undesirable consequences

- Mitigation strategies to reduce or eliminate undesirable consequences

- Monitoring of actual performance of and outcomes resulting from any new regulations

- Alteration of regulations and processes as required to bring outcomes closer to those intended

Adequate analysis and evaluation processes are entirely absent today. Not surprisingly, policy outputs tend often to be quite harmful to the nation as a whole. Such "stupid outputs" of today's political process include, but sadly are by no means limited to, the following:

- Unsupportable increases in government spending in order to buy votes

- Policies aimed at appeasing powerful domestic lobbies rather than at an achievable and/or desirable outcome for the nation as a whole

- Focusing on minor issues that have ephemeral resonance with the public (often entirely because of media manipulation) instead of addressing issues of lasting importance

- The promotion of simplistic policies that are utterly inadequate for complex issues but which have the virtue of being easy to understand and easy to "sell" to a sufficient number of voters

- The avoidance of telling hard truths to voters because politicians know such truths would be unpopular

Some parts of the world have experimented with various forms of direct democracy. Notable among these efforts have been the ballot initiatives of various US States. After a threshold of signatures has been reached in support of a given measure it automatically goes onto the ballot so that people can vote for or against it. This sounds very straightforward but in reality the implementation is deeply flawed. It's worth looking at why such attempts at representative democracy generally fail so that we can consider how to engineer a more adequate approach in future.

First of all, under the US system anyone can propose a ballot initiative. No matter how egregious the idea, provided that a sufficient number of signatures can be obtained in support it automatically goes onto the ballot. So if a religious cult believes that all people with short fingers are intrinsically evil, a ballot proposal to restrict the rights of the short-fingered can be drafted and presented to the public provided that the cult has sufficient funds to pay for signature-gathering.

Secondly, signatures in support of a proposition are generally obtained by professional organizations skilled in acquiring signatures. Hundreds of paid employees can be deployed to gather signatures outside of coffee shops, supermarkets, and other high-traffic locations where random passers-by can be inveigled for a signature in return for being left alone. Few people thus accosted take the time to familiarize themselves with the details of the proposal they are being asked to support; most often their only information comes in a highly distorted form such as "Will you help us protect children?" when the real meaning is "We want to restrict the rights of short-fingered people because we think they are evil and because they are evil they are a threat to children. Therefore we will protect children by discriminating harshly against all short-fingered people." Gathering the required number of signatures is therefore an extremely dubious method of validating the "popular appeal" of a ballot initiative.

Thirdly, once an initiative has gathered sufficient signatures to make it onto the ballot, it will be worded in such a way as to maximize confusion and obscure its real intent. An example is "This initiative is intended not to minimize the degree of restrictions that may be placed on short-fingered in order to protect our children." The organization behind the ballot utilizes extensive databases of supporter names in order to ensure that the "right" people know which way to vote; meanwhile the odds are that a significant number of people who actually oppose the measure will accidentally vote for it thanks to the highly misleading way in which it is presented.

Fourthly, although many jurisdictions require a basic cost/benefit analysis to be included along with the measure, such analyses are generally superficial and highly constrained. No one voting in 1978 for Proposition 13 in California to limit the tax on residential property was told that it would result in a huge under-funding of local services such as schools and that this under-funding would have to be made up by over-taxing young first-time home buyers in order to subsidize relatively well-off older home owners, which in turn would lead to ageing communities because younger families would be priced out of the market. Two-thirds of Californian voters approved Prop 13 and the results have been catastrophic. But, as they say, "who knew?"

From this very brief analysis we can see that the ballot initiative approach as presently instantiated is hopelessly inadequate for the purposes of satisfactory governance. Can it, however, be improved to the point where it may be rendered fit for purpose?

To begin with we can consider applying the same approach to ballot initiatives as we did to voting rights: a tiered structure based on proven qualification. The eligibility requirements that enable a person to vote can equally be used to enable that person to propose policy within the domain and at the appropriate level of city, region, or nation.

It is also evident that intentional obfuscation and misdirection has to be killed stone dead. This means we need to establish a truly neutral competent third party, and then make that third party responsible for drafting each proposal; at the very least a rigorous oversight is necessary to ensure the clearest-possible presentation of what is being suggested. We know enough about the psychology of question-framing that a good attempt can be made to avoid biasing the response through the manner in which the question is framed. An example is "Do you want to protect family values and stop government officials harassing parents following god's holy law?" which, when re-written properly becomes "Do you want to change the law to allow religious people to physically assault their children?"

Instead of paying professional signature-gatherers to stand outside supermarkets, we can leverage the Internet to send qualified citizens relevant potential initiatives so they can evaluate them and support proposals they feel have merit. In this way good ideas won't die simply because the sponsor lacks sufficient funds to pay for a small army of professional signature-gatherers. And by using validation technologies we can ensure that no one can falsify results.

As well as having a neutral third-party to draft the proposal, we need a neutral third-party to provide an adequate impact analysis: what are the likely consequences of acting on this proposal? This is always going to face the limitation of the fact that we, as a species, are notoriously poor at predicting future outcomes of present actions. Even experts generally just draw straight lines to extrapolate today into a future in which the matter of concern has increased dramatically in scale. Fortunately we have begun to make progress with computer simulations and it is likely that within a decade or two such simulations will offer a much more reliable guide than our own biases and misleading intuitions. Of course early models will be crude and error-prone but even the crudest computer simulation will be superior to our own human ability to extrapolate from current conditions. So things can only get better with regards to modeling probable outcomes and thus showing what the real-world impact of a particular proposition is likely to be.

Unlike we humans, computer programs can learn from experience and improve over time.

One last constraint is necessary. We humans often confuse personality with policy. The overwhelming reason given by US voters for putting their mark against the name of George W. Bush on the two occasions he ran for the office of US President was, "I just like the guy." Very few Republican voters could accurately enumerate even a single policy proposed by the then-candidate. Equally Bill Clinton's electoral victories were in no small measure predicated on his ability to project a "good ol' boy" persona because he knew that a great many voters would lack his enthusiasm for progressive policy and political theory and a great many more are actively turned off by anyone who appears overly intelligent.

So all policy proposals should be presented anonymously to be debated on their merits alone and not be subject to the emotional or professional biases that would inevitably arise were the identity of the proposer known to those considering the proposal. This condition of anonymity will, in some cases, be much harder to secure than one might think at first glance. But it must be achieved, otherwise groups will end up gaming the system.

If we can develop these ideas further we may be modestly confident that we can make at least a beginning. Inevitably however some will discover ways to manipulate any new system for self-advantage and therefore we have to be sure that our systems can evolve in order to respond to such challenges. It's notable that no such adaptations have occurred in representative democracies, which is why they were so easily captured by the wealthy and powerful. But if we consciously address our innate tendency to pursue self-advantage at the expense of others we can surely develop systems of governance that are to some degree self-correcting. We have, after all, been doing this in the realm of engineering for nearly two hundred years despite the initial crudity of the tools and technologies that were available to us.

We can use a simple analogy: if we think of our society as a human body, it's obvious that it will be under constant assault from pathogens. In the case of politics, the pathogens are those seeking undue influence through wealth and other powerful means. Like a virus, such people and groups subvert the body's systems to their own ends. We humans are assailed by millions of pathogens each day but for the most part we don't succumb. This is because our immune system evolves to meet each new challenge. In order to avoid capture by special interests, therefore, we need to develop systems of governance that can evolve and defeat such attempts.

This has never been tried before. It's time we began the effort.

Necessary Constraints

We humans are rather good at being unpleasant to each other and never more so when some of us have power over others. So it's essential that any system of governance should have explicit constraints in order to avoid the worst excesses of human nature. We're used to the concept of constraints as all nations have keystone laws such as the prohibitions against murder, theft, and suchlike. Now we need to extend those constraints to apply to policy overall.

Constraints with regards to governance can be framed in a general way as follows:

- Only those who have demonstrated suitable competence in a particular domain may (a) anonymously propose policy within that domain, and (b) anonymously vote upon proposals within that domain

- No law may systemically discriminate against an individual or any group of people on the basis of caste, race, political persuasion, sexuality, gender, or any other characteristic or attribute except for capability as defined by legal testing procedures

- Any person may elect to certify for any domain-specific enfranchisement at any time and there shall be no limit to the number of attempts that may be made by any person. Furthermore, once enfranchised a person may elect to recertify for the franchise at the expiry of their current period of domain-specific enfranchisement

- Each specific domain enfranchisement shall persist for five years; in the event that an individual does not recertify for the franchise upon expiry of the five-year term, that specific enfranchisement shall lapse

- No law shall impose upon any person forfeiture of life nor forfeiture of the means of sustenance, nor shall any punishment be inflicted that will cause physical pain; nor shall any relative, friend, associate or other person connected with a convicted person be in any way punished or restrained or suffer forfeiture except insofar as they too may be convicted of an offense against the law

- No individual or group shall suffer any form of collective punishment for any crime committed by an individual

- All laws shall be subject to automatic expiry at the end of ten years unless a majority of qualified citizens vote, at time of expiry, for renewal for another ten year period

The reader is encouraged to think of other constraints that should exist in order to avoid the emergence of people or groups that acquire sufficient power and influence so as to manipulate the system to their advantage at the expense of the majority.

Obviously this is a large topic; all we can do here is sketch some guidelines. In practice we would expect explicit constraints across a wide domain, much as the European Convention on Human Rights was simple in concept but detailed in practice.

So much for constraints. Now comes the question of tradeoffs.

Let's imagine a situation in which a majority of voters has approved a measure that requires the nation to spend 50% of tax revenues on supporting public education. In addition, a majority of voters has approved another measure that requires the nation to spend 40% of tax revenues on health care. Finally, a majority of voters has approved a third measure that requires the nation to spend 25% of tax revenues on infrastructure spending. In a perfectly democratic manner, the people have voted to spend 115% of total revenues.

Many readers will find it difficult to resist the temptation of saying, "That's silly, that could never happen." Well, unfortunately, this is precisely what happens today with our representative systems of government. Everywhere in the developed world governments spend more than they raise in tax revenues. They borrow the shortfall, either from international institutions like the IMF and the World Bank or more usually from capital markets by issuing government bonds.

Not surprisingly, politicians everywhere have become addicted to borrowing. It's the easiest way to buy votes and every politician is in the business of vote-buying. Eventually however the party comes crashing to an end and ordinary people are left with the broken glass, spilled ashtrays, and the mother of all hangovers. Most people know what happened to Greece; it is highly probable that Italy will also tumble off its own fiscal cliff. The subsequent social and economic disruptions accelerate the inevitable impulse toward tyranny as people clamor for "strong" leaders to save them.

Given that representative democracy has failed so signally to operate in a fiscally responsible manner, how can direct qualified democracy do better?

The first obvious point is that once we've got rid of politicians, there's no one motivated to buy votes. So a lot of nonsense policies simply never arise, which in turn means that spending requirements are smaller than they would be in representative democracies.

There are many rational ways to avoid the ever-greater-debt trap. The first is to have a firm requirement to run a balanced budget whereby revenues match or exceed expenditures rather than (as is the case today) the other way around. Those who argue *pace* Keynes that in times of recession some stimulus spending may help avert a depression can take heart from the idea that if governments run a small persistent surplus during good times then this surplus will be available for stimulus spending during hard times.

Few people would argue that it is not infinitely more prudent to spend money you already have than to borrow in order to spend money you don't have and may not be able to repay. Debt-fueled growth may seem attractive in the short term but its longer-term consequences have always been dire. We think the boom-and-bust cycles we've experienced in the West since the nineteenth century are somehow inevitable; in fact they've all been the result of excessive debt. It really is that simple because without excessive debt there's no possibility of market panic during inevitable minor economic downturns becoming a catastrophic meltdown.

Although some economists argue that nations, unlike individuals, can run perpetual debts provided that overall tax revenues are sufficient to maintain interest payments the reality is that such a situation creates (a) an intolerable liability for future generations, and (b) is acutely sensitive to fluctuations in interest rates and GDP growth rates. Spending more than we have inevitably leads to trouble; it is merely a question of when.

Another way to solve the problem of spending 115% of current revenue is to raise taxes. Jean-Baptiste Colbert, who was Minister of Finances under Louis XIV, is supposed to have said that the art of taxation is to pluck the maximum amount of feathers with the minimum amount of squawking and politicians do their best to follow this maxim by disguising taxes in a variety of creative ways. In the end, however, all taxes no matter how prettily dressed up merely serve to reduce individual purchasing power and thereby distort the economy. They also, by taking money out of people's pockets, reduce personal choice. And experience shows us clearly that no matter how much tax revenue a government raises, it will always want to spend even more.

It's salutary to recall that until the 20th century, income tax rarely exceeded ten percent and most people didn't earn enough to pay anything. Since then we've seen it rise to ninety-five percent in some countries before falling to an average of 25.5% across the club of developed nations known by the acronym OECD. Yet this figure is misleading, because on top of the supposed 25.5% comes mandatory social security charges, often as much as an additional 10% of income. And then, when we go to purchase things, there's a sales or Value Added Tax on top, sometimes as high as 23%. In many developed countries by the time you add up all the various taxes and other mandatory charges, the actual average rate of taxation exceeds 50% of take-home pay.

Even such a high level of taxation is insufficient to feed our governments' spending addiction. Governments are still locked into deficit-spending and debts are still growing. In the longer term, more taxes leads to yet more debt because economic output is depressed. This is because there's less money left over after taxes to invest in making or purchasing new products and services that create new jobs and thus more tax revenue, and this depression of output makes the mountain of debt harder to service.

Just as with bureaucratic bloat, there's no shortage of evidence for government spending bloat. A great deal of tax revenue is wasted on pointless or overly-expensive procurements; much else is squandered on things that provide little or no social utility. So it is clear that any rational form of governance needs to set explicit limits on the total percentage of GDP that can be taken from the pockets of citizens and applied to the public good.

Once the amount of revenue and spending is firmly constrained, eligible voters must vote on how best to divide up the fixed pie. For example, all approved measures can be ranked along with their costs and qualified voters can then be asked to prioritize each measure. In order to avoid the issue of trying to build quarter of a bridge or fractionalize any other all-or-nothing budget item, these items can be identified as indivisible and voted for on a yes/no basis. In other words, if measure A can either be fully funded or it's not viable, a simple majority prioritization of measure A will ensure that it gets funded while an insufficient number of votes will ensure that it does not get funded. The one flaw in this approach, obviously, is that it requires some measure of consensus to be achieved among people whose areas of qualification may be mutually exclusive. An expert in foreign policy may have little basis whereby to rank a proposed budget item created by experts in global commerce. One possible resolution may be to restrict ultimate budgetary approval to those qualified across a wider range of domains, whose ability to assess overall cost-benefit may be more adequate. We shall return to this problem shortly.

Returning to the question of resource allocation, we can note that many measures will not be indivisible. We don't make an all-or-nothing determination on schooling, for example. We agree that it is important to provide education for our children and we allocate funds to that purpose. But the funds are neither infinitely large nor infinitely small. They represent our trade-off between schooling and the many other things we must fund as a nation, such as providing a police service, a health service, a fire-suppression service, and so forth. It is not beyond the bounds of imagination to consider multiple initiatives competing for approval and subsequent funding. Equally not all expenditures must be undertaken and completed within a single budgetary period. It's perfectly reasonable to allocate 2% of total budget for each of the next three years in order to finance a large construction project or build a new naval vessel. And unlike the case with representative democracy, once a coherent and rational budget has been agreed there will be no politicians eager to play around with the budget in order to meet arbitrary goals aimed primarily at securing votes or appeasing special interests.

The Virtue of Transparency

How much should a nation spend, and what should the nation spend it on?

These apparently simple questions are in fact anything but simple. National spending priorities are a confused jumble of competing interests limited only by how much revenue can be raised through taxation and borrowing. Every government department wants more for itself, every special interest wants more for itself, and the general population want more spending on whatever people happen to believe is important at any point in time, which in turn is largely based on whatever happens to be the most recent media sensation.

Government spending resembles in many ways the annual budgeting process of large moribund corporations. Tomorrow's expenditure is based on yesterday's priorities, everyone resists giving up their piece of the pie even when circumstances have changed radically, and there is little consideration of overall cost-benefit. Unlike large moribund corporations however, nations aren't subject to hostile takeovers or investors dumping their stock. Nations can limp along for decades despite gross misallocations of budget provided special interests are appeased and citizens remain utterly unable to see through the tangled mess.

It's clear that any approach to governance that seeks to be more adequate than today's amateurish blundering must seek better solutions to the questions posed above than simply carrying on with the current approach.

This implies a great many changes, only a handful of which are obvious at this time. For example, how much should a nation spend on its prisons? This seemingly simple question is in fact very complex. In order to arrive at a reasonable answer we need to understand the influence of different types of deterrence on different types of crime. We need to understand the influence of rehabilitation on recidivism rates. We need to understand, most of all, more about the underlying causes of crime. Only when we've looked at all of these issues can we propose an initial position with regards to spending priorities within the prison system, and we must then monitor outcomes in order to be able to improve our approaches over time via the classic "learning curve."

Today such a rational approach is completely impossible. By and large we aren't interested in what works best, we're interested in satisfying our emotions. As individuals we feel the need to punish criminals, we want to feel safe by locking people away for a very long time. These simple emotions, which today are stirred up by every unscrupulous politician looking for a few easy votes, preclude any rational consideration of important factors. Once we are in a position where we can minimize calls for primitive revenge and largely ignore the uninformed notions of those unqualified to weigh in on the issue, we can slowly begin to create policies that will both reduce crime overall and reduce unnecessary spending on prisons.

Such an approach requires not only that we have the luxury of ignoring popular clamoring for more and more punishment; it also requires that results are published without being tampered with and dressed up to look better than they are. Today very few governments can resist playing with statistics in order to put a gloss on "results." Tomorrow we need to be more honest with ourselves.

This transparency is essential not only within individual domains but also across the entire field of government spending. Because all spending involves tradeoffs, it's essential that we can see the reasoning behind the tradeoffs and the outcomes that result. While this transparency may help reassure many citizens that the decisions taken were adequate, the more important reason we need transparency is to enable those who are qualified to have the best possible view of the situation. Without good data, good decision-making is impossible.

Through transparent presentation, an impartial cost/benefit analysis, and a further determination of the degree to which initiatives can be partly funded per budget period, eligible citizens can be asked explicitly to make the necessary trade-offs.

It is essential for adequate policy-making that sources of cost should be made more explicit. In the UK there is general agreement that the National Health Service (NHS) is a public good that deserves unflinching support. Anyone foolish enough to say that the NHS should be shut down would likely be lynched from the nearest lamp-post or, perhaps worse, forced to eat NHS-provided meals. Unfortunately the NHS, like all healthcare systems, faces potentially unlimited demand. As individuals continue to make very poor lifestyle choices that result in obesity-related diseases and smoking-related diseases, the sums spent on trying to help people who have willfully made themselves ill become massive and unsustainable.

By indicating sources of cost as well as potential applications of funds, qualified voters can determine the various factors involved and make more informed decisions. Let's be honest: only an intelligent and thoughtful qualified electorate could structure incentives so as to encourage beneficial behaviors and penalize behaviors that impose costs on others. No politician in a representative democracy can hope to be re-elected if they were to propose making obese people and smokers pay more or wait longer for health care because a great many voters are obese and smoke. But a qualified set of thoughtful citizens could very well understand that personal choices are influenced by personal costs and draw the obvious conclusions and thus vote for the requisite legislation to everyone's benefit including those personally unable to make more adequate lifestyle choices for themselves.

At this point it is obligatory for someone to shout "nanny state!" or an equivalent, and strenuously decry the reduction in personal liberty that such a position implies. In fact, there's no necessity for such choices to be imposed on those who do not wish to comply with socially viable policies. By way of example, the State may seek to encourage better lifestyle choices (more exercise, less junk food, fewer cigarettes smoked) by means of education and taxation but it will be up to each individual whether or not to acquiesce. Each individual is free to make their own decisions but each individual must also bear the true costs of those decisions.

Today, people who make poor lifestyle choices create a burden for others who make more adequate choices and this is surely unfair. Why should Jane, who exercises daily, eats sensibly, and who avoids consuming harmful substances, hand over huge sums for her health care coverage simply because Tom and Sally and Greg can't be bothered to exercise, consume a wide range of very unhealthy inputs, and in consequence are in a condition of permanent chronic illness for which Jane must now pay? Why should Suzie, who has looked after herself carefully all her life and is now in her seventies, have to wait years for a much-needed hip operation because the health system is blocked with thousands of obese people whose ailments are the direct result of years of careless over-eating?

At an individual level we can choose to continue to eat junk and take no exercise; we'll then simply bear the consequences of being lower down the priority list for medical attention and maybe also having to pay more for our medical treatments. This is a far more fair and equitable arrangement than exists in any nation today, and it is far more sustainable from a budget perspective. The alternative is to accept that deserving people will have to go without essential care simply because others choose to burn up limited health care resources by making themselves ill through poor lifestyle choices.

Another difference between budgets in a direct versus a representative democracy is that pork-barrel spending (spending on projects that have little intrinsic value but which can be guaranteed to deliver votes for the politician who sponsors it because it "creates employment" in the district) vanishes. Whereas certain politicians may have a strong interest in a "bridge to nowhere" or a component of a redundant yet hugely expensive new piece of military hardware or a pointless wall, it is unlikely that a majority of qualified citizens will vote for such wasteful expenditure at the cost of defunding more important measures that deliver widespread social benefit. Furthermore, unlike the horse-trading that inevitably occurs between and within political Parties in a representative democracy where the trade-offs are primarily predicated on political advantage and only secondarily (if at all) based on the nation's needs and desires, the trade-offs arising from direct democracy can't help but be far more rational and explicit.

In a qualified direct democracy there are no murky backroom deals. Everything is out on the table for everyone to examine.

All proposed new policies must be subject to economic and social cost-benefit analysis. For example, do we build a new road or a new train service? Do we invest in a better power distribution system or encourage micro-generation? Some apparently "uneconomic" policies may in fact make economic sense when seen in a larger context. By way of example, a nation could vote to provide broadband internet connections to rural locations in order to facilitate more work-from-home jobs which will reduce commuting and hence cut carbon emissions and thus reduce the cost of ameliorating climate change. The total benefit would exceed the apparent disparity between cost of provision and subsequent revenue generated from users.

Other issues are existential: does the nation wish to be able to defend itself against an aggressor, or would it prefer to surrender immediately in order to minimize loss of life?

Even though no cost-benefit analysis can truly determine overall defense spending, even such apparently "philosophical" issues are usually amenable to resolution when we take into account our innate primate behaviors. We know from overwhelming evidence that regardless of what people may believe during peacetime, the vast majority of citizens will feel an overwhelming desire to defend their territory in the face of an aggressor. The question therefore becomes simply: how best to accomplish such defensive capability?

Lest anyone feels this analysis is too facile, let's pause to contemplate the number of occasions in history when the vast majority of those within a defined geography have elected to submit to invasion and pillage without offering any resistance.

Not easy, is it? And the very few examples one might cite turn out to be bogus: people did resist, they were exterminated by the invaders, and the invaders then air-brushed the resisters out of history in support of the "peaceful civilizing mission" story so common among empire-builders.

The fact is we evolved to defend our group's territory because this was the behavior that resulted in increased odds of survival and hence increased odds of passing on the genes that code for this behavior. Any early proto-humans who rolled over and accepted invasion were eradicated and their pacifist genes largely fell out of the gene pool. It's not a question of morality or ethics; it's just basic genetics. Evolution doesn't care whether we're happy or sad, it doesn't care about our beliefs; evolution is merely whatever keeps genes in the gene pool.

We don't have to believe that every single person in a society will want to stand and fight, nor that the desire to stand and fight is philosophically "right" or "wrong." We just see that empirical evidence shows that a majority of people will feel this way, the feeling is consistent with evolutionary forces, and this behavior must therefore be factored into our idea of how defense policy should be formulated. We must accommodate reality and not believe that any philosophical position, no matter how beautifully argued, will predominate over hardwired instincts. History shows us that for every Bertrand Russell there will be ten thousand eager youths ready to fight an aggressor.

And let's face it: if this wasn't the case, life would be even easier for wannabe tyrants. So there's a strong moral case to be made for resistance as well. So it's apparent that even the most peace-oriented State will need to budget something in order to achieve a credible defense posture. This is especially true in a world in which the Pax Americana is no more. No nation is ever likely to rewrite its national anthem so that the first words are "All praise to the glorious invaders of <our country's name here>."

Our final question then is: how best to divide the money available? Solutions to this problem are still in their infancy but we do have at least some places to begin. Linear regression was developed to enable company managers to determine near-optimal production quantities based on the near-optimal mix of inputs, assuming some prior knowledge of demand. It is not beyond our imagination to consider that if each domain (education, defense, health care, infrastructure, etc.) has a cost-benefit curve that these multiple curves can be combined via a linear programming analysis to yield a near-optimal mix. So for example X is spent on defense because this is the optimal amount relative to (a) overall defensive capability, and (b) overall social benefit.

This is obviously a very simplistic notion but as our computational and mathematical capabilities continue to develop, we can be cautiously optimistic about continuous improvement. Our alternative is today's chaotic and unreasonable situation in which too often vast sums are spent with very little to show because there is no coherent decision-making process other than "what can we sell to a sufficient number of voters in order to secure our re-election?" So any more rational and transparent approach to the allocation of resources is bound to be dramatically superior to our current situation. We don't have to achieve perfection on Day One; we just need to do better than we're doing today and then improve from there.

The concept of creating feedback loops to enable continuous learning and continuous improvement is essential. Any system of qualified democracy will have significant flaws, not just budgetary issues, when initially implemented. There must be explicit mechanisms whereby qualified democracy can be subject to continuous assessment and improvement.

One huge challenge is to manage our innate human tendency to want simple answers. We're hardwired to seek simplicity because back on the savannah simple worked best. Unfortunately in a modern complex world simple answers are a one-way path to disaster. Nowhere is this more true today than in the sound-bites we're bombarded with every minute of every day.

Yet there can be no simple answers, and very often the answers to today's problems can only be discovered by means of innovative thinking tomorrow. This brings us to another crucial observation: for a society to thrive and improve, innovation must not be squashed.

In recent years many economists have attempted to understand why innovation and growth occur in some parts of the world but not in others. They have built complex models to show, for example, that population size may be a key determinant. The logic here is that the more people you have, the greater the probability of an innovator being among them and then the larger the available market for innovative products. Other models presume access to navigable waterways are an essential precondition for economic growth because they enable trade to occur over wide distances. Unfortunately all of these models are specious and fail to fit the available historical data. For every example it is possible to find counter-examples where the supposed enabler has had no noticeable effect. We have in fact only one example of astonishing innovation and high growth and rather than attempting to play games with complex spreadsheets it is far more useful to look at the example we have and attempt to understand it.

Our question is: why did innovation and then extraordinary economic growth occur in a few small and otherwise negligible northern European countries commencing around five hundred years ago? Why did mass innovation not occur instead in a country like China with its large population and stable system of government? Or in India with its navigable Ganges to ease trade across vast distances?

It turns out the answer lies in the matter of privilege. Whenever a society unduly privileges certain segments over others, innovation is smothered. This is because the privileged segments will act to maintain their own interests above all else and such interests could be threatened by any significant innovation that may enable other segments to become more important. Privileged segments of society will also control information flows to ensure few if any members of the general population will have sufficient knowledge to see the big picture.

What does this mean in practice? If we look at Europe in the fifteenth century we see a patchwork of nations and city-states, kings and emperors and local barons and a few ultra-wealthy merchants. Sitting above all, however, was the Pope. The head of the Roman Catholic Church commanded power greater than any European monarch. And the primary interest of the Church was to maintain its position. Whenever new thought, which is the precursor to innovation, arose the Church reliably quashed it. When Giordano Bruno proposed that the Earth orbits the Sun, he was burned alive. When Galileo Galilei likewise said that his observations through his telescope confirmed that

71

the Earth orbits the Sun, he was threatened with torture and confined to house arrest. These are the famous examples; thousands more individuals were suppressed in similar manner.

The net result was that the Catholic Church smothered ideas and innovation for hundreds of years. Why did this baleful condition not continue into the present day? When Martin Luther in 1517 nailed his ninety-five protesting theses to the door of the Wittenberg Castle church he accidentally set off a process that in Northern Europe shattered the omnipresent power of the Catholic Church. Protestantism quickly fragmented into dozens of different sects as it spread. In southern Europe the Catholic Church was able to resist the advance of Protestantism but in the north it took root and spread in many forms. But each sect was comparatively small and powerless. No sect, with the temporary exception of Calvinism in Switzerland, could dominate society and crush new thoughts in the way the Catholic Church could still do in southern Europe. And so it became possible for the first time in a thousand years for individuals to begin to think more freely. People were more able to question supposed eternal verities, they were able to innovate and create and adopt new technologies and these technologies in turn spurred new discoveries and therefore more new thinking in what we now recognize as a classic feed-forward loop.

Meanwhile in China thought was controlled by the powerful State. Indian theological attitudes resulted in acquiescence to the status quo, no matter how dysfunctional. Although a few in India made important contributions to mathematics the religious posture of passivity in the face of destiny meant that no meaningful social innovation occurred. In the Arab world, although a brief scientific efflorescence occurred in mathematics and astronomy, the emphasis on rote-learning the Koran and an unquestioning acceptance of its religionist worldview meant that no lasting social innovations could occur.

Only in the fragmented religious environment of western Europe could innovative thinking and technological innovation thrive. And thus relatively small and obscure countries such as the Netherlands and the Great Britain slowly began to innovate. Slowly their economies began to grow until by the eighteenth century these small nations were at the forefront of social and economic development. No Church or all-powerful State could crush James Watt on the grounds that his Rocket was heretical or threatened the harmony of the State bureaucracy. No Church or all-powerful State could imprison Michael Faraday, whose research ultimately enabled much of today's electronics technology. And when in the late eighteenth century the North American colonies broke from the British Crown they carried with them the same freedom to think new thoughts and create new technologies because there was no overwhelming dominant religious or State institution to crush anyone with the temerity to challenge the status quo.

It is apparent, therefore, that transparency of ideas and the freedom to think differently from what has been thought in the past is central to any society's ability to improve over time. As we consider modes of governance and the goals we wish to pursue we need always to remember that stasis is the enemy of improvement. New ideas need to come into existence and have the chance to spread. Most bad ideas will ultimately be rejected while many good ideas will often (but not always) be developed further. The only constraint is that our ideas must be based on reality, not on wishes beliefs. Our ideas must reflect facts, not assertions. Provided this simple distinction is maintained, transparency of ideas means a greater probability of continued social and economic growth. We cannot afford to return to a condition wherein one or more powerful special interests suppresses new thinking in order to maintain its own advantages. It is striking that even today, hundreds of years after the Reformation in Europe, southern Europe still lags its northern neighbors in terms of innovation and social equality. The ability of the dead hand of religion to crush the life out of a society should never be underestimated.

Infotainment: the Cholera of Today

It is not much of an exaggeration to say that much of what is promulgated today across the Internet, television channels, and print newspapers is the mental equivalent of sewage. And just as pumping raw sewage into people's homes would result in diseases like cholera, so pumping raw mental sewage into people's minds results in diseases like populism and nationalism.

Today the mass media feeds and amplifies our belief that for every problem there is a quick and easy answer, because the media knows what its audience wants. Like fast-food outlets giving us junk food, the mass media gives us junk ideas. And when the media presents us with a new scandal we believe we deserve an immediate response. *They* must do something about it! Now! And then tomorrow there will be a new scandal which will require immediate action; we'll forget about what we were so agitated about today. In consequence we come to feel we live in a world of never-ending threats and crises about which *they* seem powerless to do anything. We're all chasing our own tails in a never-ending cycle of anxiety and helplessness.

This harmful mental sewage isn't confined to so-called "news" media. It's in every piece of entertainment we watch. Hollywood in particular spews out mental pollution on a daily basis. How many junk movies have titillated audiences with a sexy femme-fatale who then (of course) turns out to be a serial killer and who invariable meets a bad end? The message: sex is dangerous unless you're using it to sell product.

How many junk movies have employed the same old tired clichés over and over and over again, clichés that merely reinforce worn-out stereotypes such as how helpless males are when forced to care for a small child or how emotional women are when dealing with life's inevitable problems? And of course we have the endless "action" movies that show how even the most complex problem can be resolved with a gun.

When we encourage junk food outlets on every street corner, it's no surprise people become obese. Today over eighty-five percent of US citizens are overweight and most Europeans aren't far behind. The moment McJunk appears on the high street, obesity follows. We're being harmed even more by the junk infotainment we endlessly consume on our televisions, our tablets, and our phones.

Which means we now have to start thinking very carefully indeed about what kind of media landscape can help rather than harm us. We have to break the distorting mirror and replace it with something better.

One very striking aspect of Western societies since World War II has been the role of the mass media in fomenting discontent, spreading misinformation, and in general shaping the attitudes and beliefs of hundreds of millions of citizens. Without a free press to expose wrongdoing among elected politicians and powerful private citizens, a nation may more readily be captured by those with ill intent. Yet a "free" press necessarily must be paid for and thus each newspaper and radio station and television channel and Internet website and podcast is competing for an audience in order to sell subscriptions and win advertising revenue.

The most successful media enterprises are those that pander to prejudice and reinforce ignorance. Even when the mass media isn't intentionally distorting issues or stirring up atavistic impulses, its endless quest for attention means that it will always give prominence to the sensational over the meaningful. When Donald Trump was competing in the Republican primaries throughout 2016 the media gave him billions of dollars of free publicity simply because he was an absurd buffoon. Whereas the other contenders for the Party's nomination sought to project competence and seriousness, Trump was an infantile halfwit who said unbelievably stupid and offensive things. Trump was, in other words, a freak show and a great many people like to gawp at freaks. Deprived of the traveling circus with its Bearded Lady, Dog Woman, and Incredible Midget, the world turns to its screens. Those providing content for the screens know that freaks appeal to the masses. In consequence 85% of media coverage focused solely on Trump because this drew eyeballs and eyeballs means advertising revenue. And because we are group primates for whom ubiquity means authority, millions of people voted for Trump for the simple reason that his was the face they instantly recognized and his were the sound-bites they could most easily remember.

The USA thus became the first nation in history to destroy itself for the sake of advertising revenue.

Meanwhile the insidious influence of the mass media continues to be felt across a wide spectrum of issues. A great many people believe that all genetically modified foods are magically "bad" and that vaccines cause autism and that fast-food chains adulterate their products with "goo."

Sometimes falsehoods are generated through ignorance and misunderstanding; at other times they are generated intentionally. The egregious and repellent Fox News organization is focused entirely on fabricating stories, whipping viewers into a hysteria of fear, and then presenting them with adverts. Its motto really ought to be "Proudly Destroying Democracy by Lying to the Simple-Minded Since 1996." In recent years the Kremlin has pioneered social disruption in the West by generating endless memes that are intended to create discord, confusion, doubt, and fear. It's a simple formula: pump out hundreds of such memes every week and a few will gain traction; invest in further promoting these and soon you'll have captured the minds of millions.

Every British person re-tweeting or re-posting a meme about how the Irish backstop is unnecessary because Switzerland borders on five other countries is doing the Kremlin's work for it. Every person in the West who repeats a "patriotic" meme is doing the Kremlin's work for it. And none of us realizes we're being played for dupes. We think we're being "patriotic" or "smart." Of course it helps the Kremlin that some of these divisive memes are home-grown. The dregs of the mass media is always happy to create division because nothing appeals to the simple-minded more than simple-minded polarities. The mass media doesn't care that it's destroying society; it's just looking to maximize this week's ad revenues.

All of which just goes to show how not-smart we humans really are.

In consequence of so much misinformation coming from such a disparate and motley array of sources, we have so many fallacious beliefs that it would take an entire book just to list them. This awful distortion is aided by the fact that research shows we humans absorb simple but wrong information far more readily than actual facts; we also pass on such false information more eagerly than any truthful information. This is all because our primate brains, evolved to cope with the relatively simple world of the savannah and the primordial forests, really don't like trying to engage with complexity. Reality overwhelms our capabilities and no one likes feeling overwhelmed.

We're thus easy prey for the false choices beloved of media organizations the world over. How many trash newspaper banners have we seen demanding that no X shall be provided for Z until A has been provided for B? To take just a few examples from recent times, we've seen UK media chains demanding that no Syrian refugees should be housed until there are no ex-British Army personnel living on the streets. No foreign aid should be given until every British pensioner gets assistance with their winter heating bills. No foreigners should be allowed into Britain until every Briton has a job. This sort of false dichotomy helped lead the British to Brexit, which is a policy guaranteed to destroy millions of jobs, wreck the economy, and hugely diminish British quality of life. But promoting such simple-minded nonsense did generate a lot of advertising revenue, which was its only purpose.

In many developed countries there is also an obsession in the media for reporting "both sides of the story." Whereas in real life there are rarely two sides to any story (there is the truth, and then there is no shortage of alternative views), the media creates the impression of equality between fact and fiction. This false equivalence then permeates society.

In the USA many States require schools to teach both evolution and creationism on the grounds that students must be exposed to "both sides." Yet a moment's thought shows that no society is served by pretending that a highly powerful explicatory account of real-world facts is equivalent to the creation myth of a tribe of goat-herders who lived over three thousand years ago. Moreover, why should one particular creation myth be regarded as "the other side of the story?" There are hundreds of creation myths available. Surely if we're going to give "the other side of the story" we should teach children as many creation myths as we can? But apparently there are always only two sides to any story. Any more sides than two would confuse far too many people who, let's face it, are already terminally confused.

Do we really want to live in a world where the great mass of people are being fed a stream of endless lies and distortions? But if we want to avoid censorship, which is readily abused by the influential and powerful, how can we reduce the harm done by unfettered communications while retaining as much as possible of the benefits? Should we adopt the Chinese model in which the state censors and suppresses everything it deems unsuitable for the general population? Or should we accept that we're always fools and if there's money to be made or power to be gained from misleading us then this is merely another inevitable fact of life?

This is obviously not an easy question to address. All groups and societies create their own information flows and even when state censorship is at its most extreme, individuals find ways to convey information to like-minded others. In the Soviet Union dissidents developed *samizdat* publishing and doubtless dissident Chinese are finding ways to express their views in ways that stand some chance of out-maneuvering the censors. For the most part, however, the great mass of people will be content with whatever is foisted upon them. If you doubt this, just turn on a television anywhere in the world for five minutes. So it's essential for any well-meaning society to understand the power of communications technologies and attempt to harness this power for positive ends rather than permit it to be abused in the service of the powerful and the irresponsible.

In order to see possible solutions to our information problem we need to consider what our aims are. It is right and proper that citizens should have access to truthful and reliable information. Even under a capitalist economy altruistic websites can survive, albeit precariously. Wikipedia is the oft-cited yet sadly almost unique example of such survival. Precisely because Wikipedia is the exception rather than the rule we can deduce that a capitalist economy is unlikely of itself to give rise to many such sources of relatively unbiased and accurate information. On the other side of the scale we see far too many examples of rabble-rousing masquerading as "news" or "current affairs" or "political opinion."

Rupert Murdoch is today's pre-eminent exemplar of capitalism without morality. Murdoch's various media enterprises have a single goal: to churn out as much cash as possible week after week in order to service his debt burden. The easiest way to achieve this goal is to target less intellectually capable citizens in the nations in which Murdoch controls media properties and feed them simple-minded lies and distortions. Other media groups such as Sinclair Broadcast Group have learned this lesson well and are using the tactics crafted at Fox News and The Sun to great effect. Meanwhile the Disney Corporation spews out a never-ending stream of content designed to pander to and thereby reinforce popular prejudices ranging from gender stereotypes (women are either "the feisty girl" or helpless creatures needing to be rescued, while men are invariably heroic) to Prozac-filled parodies of once-loved characters created by the likes of A.A. Milne and Rudyard Kipling.

It's clear that we can't permit unregulated media to poison the discourse of civil society. Yet if we close down all the media properties and censor the Internet we are likely to find ourselves on a fool's errand. People want information and reliable information is a cornerstone of any society wishing to be able to maintain progress towards desirable goals. If we did not know about global warming we would be less likely to seek solutions to the problem; if we were unaware of malfeasance in high places we would be less likely to demand accountability and reform. As we can't un-invent the Internet we are highly unlikely to be able to suppress information flows, and those flows may be tainted in the same manner as today's endless spew of misinformation and lies.

If the State will tend to distort media output in order to reinforce its own dominance and if private enterprises will tend to distort media output in order to maximize advertising revenue, we obviously need to look for a different model. Our ideal media model should be free of the risk of state capture and should not rely on income generated by sensationalism.

We do have some partial examples to draw upon. The British Broadcasting Corporation in the UK and the Canadian Broadcasting Corporation in Canada are indicators of how we may solve our general problem, at least within a limited domain. Both these exemplars suffer from fundamental systemic flaws, but the flaws can be addressed. For example the BBC is funded by the UK government by means of a license fee payable by every household that owns a television set. This now-antiquated model provided a reasonably stable form of income. Yet the problems are obvious: because the money is relayed to the BBC via the UK government there is always some risk of assumed government interference. Worse still, the BBC has since its inception been hopelessly confused about its purpose. Its *raison d'etre* is to supply the high-quality content that commercial organizations would be unlikely to supply; in other words, the BBC's role is to compensate for market failure by providing truthful and intellectually stimulating content. Yet because the license fee falls on all households the BBC has persuaded itself that it must simultaneously justify this fee by providing lowbrow content of the sort enjoyed by the masses and already provided in bulk by commercial organizations. This makes most of the BBC's spending wasteful and pointless. And as more and more people get their information primarily from the Internet, a television-license-based revenue model is doomed to extinction. So if we want to propose solutions to our current "information dilemma" we must not blindly follow the path of the BBC.

We can imagine a world in which, at least in developed nations aiming at constructive and peaceful civic discourse, news organizations are funded by means of an independent body supported by taxation just as schools, clean water, roads and other public goods are funded today. When we consider that when we move beyond representative democracy we will have no elected politicians who could exert pressure on such an independent body, high-quality information-rich programming could be achieved and sustained. Indeed it is essential for the adequate functioning of any modern society; a major reason for the spread of populism/nationalism in recent years has been precisely the absence of adequate information and the prominence of simple-minded lies and distortions.

Today more than forty percent of US citizens get their primary "news" from social media such as Facebook. Most of that information is woefully inaccurate and much of it is simply propaganda. Facebook's algorithms ensure that citizens increasingly live in an information bubble inside which they are fed more of what the algorithm knows they want to hear. Many people want to hear lies. This is obviously a disaster for civic society but fortunately the remedy is not difficult to imagine. We already have laws in place that encourage corporations toward responsible behavior. In developed nations a chemical manufacturer would be subject to punitive fines and other damages were it to discharge noxious chemicals into the surrounding environment. Shops that sell unsafe foods are likewise subject to penalties. If we extend such normal protections into the realm of the Internet we can reduce the amount of harm presently experienced. Social media companies cannot claim unique exemption merely because the harm they can cause is mental rather than physical. All pollution is damaging to society and must therefore be subject to stringent regulation. And while Internet companies have global reach but their servers are located outside the jurisdiction of most nations, it's technically not particularly difficult these days to block content from servers that are the source of malicious data.

One may legitimately ask: what would be the basis of deciding whether or not a blog post or meme should be regarded as polluting civic society? While a complete exploration of this topic will require a book of its own, we can here briefly sketch the essence of a reply. Information should be in accordance with recognized facts; information should be presented in an emotionally neutral manner; and arguments should be internally consistent. So for example one would not be permitted to claim "most crimes are committed by immigrants." Nor would one be permitted to state "An evil wave of immigrants is coming to undermine the fabric of our society and corrupt our children." And one could not propose that immigrants are "living idly off the State" while simultaneously "stealing our jobs."

Lies succeed when they are repeated. Sadly today's media organizations have become little more than conduits for the lies spewed out by tyrants, demagogues, and infantile blusterers. Reform is thus essential.

We need to extend our existing consumer protection laws to require social media organizations (a) to preclude publication of propaganda and misinformation, and (b) to publish only information which is supported by available knowledge and facts. If some infantile orange halfwit tells a lie, it's not reported but instead true statements are sent out into the world. Any social media used to promulgate the blusterer's lies will be subject to penalty; this will result in the blusterer being deprived of a platform by means of which to spread lies and hatred. A voice reduced to a whisper will not so readily triumph over truth. Instead of asking social media organizations to take down false statements we must ask them to block those making such statements. While individuals may masquerade under a variety of noms-de-plume, it is a little more difficult to masquerade under a variety of IP addresses. Furthermore, as AI systems continue to improve we can begin to utilize computers to identify and automatically delete posts containing factually incorrect information or inflammatory statements.

Lest anyone protest that governments (or society as a whole) has no business imposing regulations that reduce the profits of corporations, we can note that this is in fact precisely one of the functions of governance, albeit usually imperfectly performed because corporations have undue influence over easily-bought politicians.

For example DuPont and General Motors conspired to introduce lead into petrol back in 1924 simply because they owned the patent for lead tetraethyl and would make billions as a result even though they knew it would cause widespread lead poisoning among those inhaling automobile exhaust gases. Belatedly, fifty years later, governments began introducing legislation to phase out the use of leaded petrol. The health of citizens eventually came to matter more than the profits of DuPont.

Likewise the large tobacco companies knew for decades that their products killed consumers; eventually Western governments slowly began to regulate cigarettes in order to reduce the enormous cost of treating unnecessary cancers, emphysema and other smoking-related diseases.

Society has a legitimate interest in restricting the ability of corporations to pursue profits when such profits are obtained through causing harm to members of society. Today we fail to grasp the concept of mental pollution; tomorrow people will look back on Fox News and Briebart with the same revulsion we feel today when we view pictures of maimed and soot-blackened infant chimney-sweeps from the late Victorian period.

These suggestions only impact the mainstream: formal news and large-scale social media. But in a world in which any individual can create a popular blog or a website or garner Twitter followers by spouting nonsense, what can we do about the Internet in general?

What should have been an enormous social good has turned out to be for the most part a river carrying mental sewage. What can a civil society do to reduce the amount of flotsam and toxic waste carried on the back of an endless flood of TCP/IP packets? While it would be nice to imagine we can extend the notion of "polluter pays" to cover individual productions the reality is different. Anyone can create a blog or website on any server anywhere in the world. While technology can be used to block a lot of malicious content, it will never stop one hundred percent.

Fortunately we do not need to engineer total effectiveness in any policy designed to reduce the worst aspects of Internet-based communications. Most people get most of their "information" from providers located in their home nation or from a few global companies who likewise source content locally. This means that penalties can be effective despite their theoretical shortcomings. For example Breibart News may locate its servers in Russia or Venezuela but their contributors live in the USA and (to a much lesser extent) in a couple of other Western nations. It is highly unlikely that Breibart contributors are sufficiently motivated to exile themselves for years in insalubrious locations merely in order to continue to spew out misinformation and hate-filled propaganda. Those few individuals who decide to exile themselves will doubtless have plenty of time to consider the wisdom of their choice as they queue for basics like toilet paper and lament their inability to fly home to visit family and friends.

All of these remedies presuppose the ability to distinguish fact from propaganda, truth from lies, and accurate information from unintentional disinformation. Yet we live in a world of imperfect knowledge and science is perpetually uncovering new information that may sometimes upturn previously held notions. How can we deal with the inherent ambiguity of knowledge in order to make judgements about what information is useful because it is accurate and what information is harmful because it is false?

We can begin by setting some basic criteria. First of all, new information must be fact-checked against the existing repository of knowledge. Sources must be evaluated for credibility. For example, the claims of an obscure researcher whose experimental design is flawed and whose data is suspicious cannot be regarded in the same light as the claims of a respected research team whose experimental design meets the required standards and whose data has been published for everyone to review and replicate.

Secondly, information must be assessed relative to social benefit. While it is no doubt pleasing for certain media organizations to manufacture public outrage by publishing anecdotal stories in which a single unrepresentative asylum-seeker obtains social housing while a single unrepresentative ex-soldier is denied social housing, it is of far greater relevance to the nation that its large capital assets such as battleships are incapable of defending themselves due to procurement budget misallocation. Or to put it another way, each potential news item needs to be assessed in terms of its impact on the nation. While a terrorist incident that kills a score of civilians at a pop concert is indeed an atrocity, we need to remember that twice that many died on the same day in regular traffic accidents caused by ordinary human incompetence.

Today's "news" focuses almost exclusively on negative events. A terrorist event or airplane crash or celebrity break-up is far more captivating for the average citizen than news about a trade deal that will ultimately improve their lives beyond recognition. Yet our societies are shaped far more by matters of importance than by transient scandals and atypical deaths. We know that when bombarded with negative news, people become fearful and support repressive measures that serve mainly to make matters worse, rather than support policies that are coherent and provide long-term benefit.

Of course a great many people do not want meaningful information. Many citizens wish merely to distract themselves with sports and celebrity gossip and similar ephemera. For such people it will be necessary to churn out harmless but diverting nonsense by means of which they can distract themselves temporarily from the vicissitudes of their own lives. But even here we must be mindful of the sorts of distraction we provide: harmless nonsense is very different from vicious character-assassination. So-called "reality TV" and shock-jock radio stations aren't harmless entertainment: they are mental toxins. As such, they cannot be allowed in any society that aspires to adequacy.

Even within a system of governance that ensures only the informed and thoughtful are permitted a voice in matters of importance, the general disposition of the great mass of uninformed people is vital for civic order and a prerequisite for a humane society. Thus our entertainments should be factual, informative, educative, and promote desirable characteristics instead of merely being whatever mental pollution happens to attract the most eyeballs because it is the intellectual equivalent of junk food: loaded with things that are instantly appealing but which induce significant long-term harm.

While we will never be able to stop the flood of idle chatter and misinformation transmitted through the Internet, we can in meaningful ways provide more adequate information flows and discredit the untruths that will perpetually circulate in search of the credulous and intellectually indolent. No solution to the problem of misinformation can be perfect, but our societies deserve far greater effort and intellectual focus than they have hitherto received. We also need to realize we can use a variety of tools to assist us. Most people follow their feelings rather than engage in complex ratiocination. Therefore, when looking to combat misinformation, we need to use emotion rather than reason. If the US media had resolutely mocked Donald Trump instead of amplifying his nonsense and if the overall message was "you'd have to be really, really stupid to vote for this buffoon" it's unlikely he'd have secured nearly sixty-three million votes. Likewise if Brexiteers had been ridiculed and their lies held up for scorn, far fewer people would have voted for Brexit and the UK would have been spared massive self-inflicted damage.

It is clear we cannot continue to permit the status quo, any more than we permitted the continuation of child labor or child pornography. People often like things that are very harmful for them and even the most liberal society must intervene to prevent large-scale and persistent self-damage. There is no difference in principle between banning smoking in public places and banning knowingly false or intentionally negative "news." Although today it is implausible to imagine any government attempting to regulate the media and much less having the competence to do so successfully, we must hope that a more thoughtful generation will see how information intimately impacts governance and therefore how important it is to ensure that information is factual and germane.

Values and Changes

We now need to ask what values we believe are most fair and most efficacious for the overall well-being of everyone in society regardless of wealth or status, for these values will guide not only our information policies but our social policies in general.

At first it might seem that stability is a pre-eminent value. After all, none of us much likes having our lives disrupted. We strive for predictability in our own lives; surely this should be a goal for any worthwhile society?

In fact, stability is impossible. In nature evolution drives constant change. In our own human societies we have multiple forces acting against stasis. Just as the much-vaunted "harmony of nature" is a specious concept held only by people who spend very little time in the natural world so too we have to accept that attempting to maintain any status quo over any meaningful period of time is likewise an erroneous notion. Everything is in flux, all the time. The question for us is: how do we harness the forces of change so as to minimize adverse impacts and maximize beneficial outcomes?

While highly militarized societies like ancient Sparta or the twentieth-century USSR may be stable for a few decades they impose huge emotional costs on individuals, suppress innovation and improvement, and require a high rate of oppression. Few people in the developed world would wish for their children to live in such societies. So we must specify a minimum set of characteristics essential to secure appropriate individual liberties from which all other good aspects of society ultimately spring. This was the intention of the US Constitution and its various Amendments and while the American body politic has not aged well we can still admire the goals of the Founding Fathers even as we acknowledge their many limitations and the Constitution's many weaknesses.

We must above all accept what is practically possible given the constraints of our evolved behaviors. Utopia isn't within our grasp. We're a primate group species with hardwired behaviors that militate against purely rational actions. Just as kangaroos can't fly, we can't behave rationally. We're driven by emotions over which we have very limited control and we see our world through a very narrow aperture in consequence of the way our brains are hardwired. So we have to define adequacy in terms of both desirable *and* achievable outcomes.

At this point we need to address the inevitable charge of "elitism" that is nowadays thrown at anyone who has the audacity to suggest that greater competence would be a good thing. The arguments against "elitism" are generally as follows: firstly, elitism enables capture of resources by the fortunate at the expense of the less fortunate; and secondly that the concept of elitism psychologically harms those who aren't counted among the "elite." If society could eliminate "elites" everyone remaining would thereafter be much happier.

Or to put it another way, anti-elitism is just age-old envy and resentment wrapped up in modern jargon.

Amid all the talk of "elites" it's rarely noticed that we haven't really bothered to define what we mean by the word. There's a general notion that if you're rich you're a member of "the elite" but a moment's thought shows this to be silly. Most wealthy people simply inherited their head start in life. That doesn't make them "elite." It just makes them members of what Warren Buffet has memorably termed "the lucky sperm club."

A better definition of "elite" means: someone who has achieved significant mastery of their domain. It's obvious that we expect and require elitism in all meaningful areas of human life. In fact elites are everywhere, in every part of life. "The elite" does not exist as a tiny monolithic group. Tom is a member of the technology elite because he knows how to set up corporate computer networks; Mary is a member of the medical elite because she is a skilled urologist; Kamal is a member of the elite because he is a structural engineer; and Sephida is a member of the elite because she leads a team developing software for DNA sequencing machines. Sephida does not have her feelings hurt because Kamal was responsible for constructing the facilities in which she works, nor does Tom feel diminished in consequence of Mary treating him for kidney disease.

The notion that "the elite" is necessarily harmful to the many is clearly false. Yet we continue to speak about an "elite" largely because journalists and demagogues lazily conflate wealth and influence with elitism but a moment's thought reveals the obvious: there are a great many wealthy individuals who are so intellectually impoverished and possessed of such inadequate personalities that equating them with any notion of "elite" is laughable. By chance or by theft they have acquired wealth but that is all they have. Such people make no positive contribution to society and so they're essentially worthless. Far from being elite they are hollow creatures whose passing will go unmarked and who will be forgotten in mere days. We remember Bacon, Copernicus, Galileo, Newton, Pasteur, Mozart, Beethoven, Nightingale, Curie, Tchaikovsky, Prokofiev, Mendeleev, Einstein, Planc, Heisenberg, and so many others for the contributions they made to humankind. Meanwhile absurdities like Trump and his family will be remembered if at all merely as a footnote, an illustration of abject inadequacy in every regard.

Investment bankers, pop personalities, entertaining politicians and other transient parasites are "elite" merely in the sense that they are wealthy or appear frequently in the mass media. But real elitism is a quite separate concept. And while it is true that wealth can buy disproportionately access to good schooling and a few other advantages it is notable that even educational institutions desperate for donations continue to seek out bright students among the less well-off in order to ensure the perpetuation of their academic status. No university can afford for long to be regarded merely as a dumping-ground for the dim-witted scions of the transiently wealthy.

Likewise there are a great many forms of influence but attempting to apply the label "elite" is unwise, for what is "elite" about media journalists chasing sensationalist stories or business people lobbying for favorably distorted regulations? Or do we mean by "elite" those citizens who are educated to university level? If so, then as today the majority of young people in the developed nations go on to higher education this implies that the majority is "the elite" and so the concept evaporates in a puff of self-evident absurdity.

Instead of getting tangled in silly abstractions and age-old resentments, we must begin with empirical observation when it comes to thinking carefully about what we need to value most highly in our societies.

Like most animals we have evolved to want to protect our young so we feel distress when we exist under conditions whereby such protection may not adequately be extended. How many of us would be content to live in places where our children may easily be killed by a stray bullet, a barrel bomb, any passing armed insurgent, or by religious or government edict? How many of us would be content to see our children condemned to grinding manual labor and strictly precluded from earning their living in any less arduous manner? How many of us would be content to see our children die from curable disease simply because our government has decided that medicines are unnecessary or a "trick?" These aren't idle questions: they refer to the lives of hundreds of millions of people who didn't have the good fortune to be born in the West.

If we're honest with ourselves it's clear that the vast majority of us will prefer to live in societies where security of life and opportunity of occupation are the norm rather than the exception. We need not concern ourselves with abstract musings about utility or the greater good; we can simply extrapolate from our hardwired instincts and desires that selection pressure has caused to evolve and persist within every one of us. We may be largely unaware of our hardwired behaviors and exist rather like machines blindly executing a program; we certainly do not for the most part analyze our behaviors abstractly and dispassionately. We usually pretend to ourselves that we have "free will" (which is in fact a meaningless concept) but in reality we're hardwired by evolution to behave in predictable ways under particular circumstances. The fact that we're unaware of these limitations doesn't alter the fact of their existence.

When we look over the field of anthropology we see a few major trends, all of which have clear evolutionary origins.

The first major trend is that violence decreases as wealth can be abstracted. A brief thought experiment shows why. Let's imagine Mika, a young hunter-gatherer living some 30,000 years ago. Mika is two years past puberty and because life is precarious he may not have many years available in which to achieve reproductive success. But females require proofs of fitness and most especially proofs that indicate there will be resources available for any offspring that results from copulation. Mika doesn't have a lot of time to acquire resources, but he definitely wants to mate.

One option is to take someone else's resources. Unfortunately for Mika, other males will be unwilling to relinquish any assets they've accumulate for precisely the same reasons Mika wants them: they represent mating opportunities and potentially a longer life. If he wants to take something, Mika must use force. We see this type of behavior in every society where abstraction of wealth is impossible. The cattle raids among the Ma'asai people in Kenya and the dawn raids of the Yanomamo in the Amazon rainforest are holdovers from our evolutionary history. The potential cost is very significant but the potential gains are just as large.

Our ancestors attempted to reduce violence by means of tribal laws that discouraged certain behaviors they had identified as leading to great harm and social disruption. As best as we can tell, all societies have had laws regarding theft and assault and all mythologies contain elements of such laws. Unfortunately, as we all know, laws are not particularly effective in modifying or suppressing behavior especially when the stakes (reproductive success) are so high. They are, to use the old phrase, more honored in the breach than in the observation.

Conversely, when wealth can be abstracted there is less utility in assault. Whereas our ancestor Mika might have been able to steal the greater portion of another man's assets

30,000 years ago when those assets comprised some stored dried roots and perhaps a tethered animal, today our assets are abstracted in a variety of ways, the most obvious of which is through bank accounts where wealth is what appears on a ledger. So there is far less incentive to attack wealthy people because the gains will be relatively minor (a wallet, a wristwatch) compared to the potential cost.

Potential cost brings up a second characteristic: the abstraction of revenge. In tribal societies the high risk of violence means that closely-related individuals will tend to band together to protect each other against other bands of closely-related individuals. An attack on one person may be revenged by his entire group while the transgressor will likewise be defended by his entire group in turn. From this basic interaction we get the generations-long feuds seen in backward places such as Sicily and the Appalachian Mountains, in addition to every tribal society known to anthropologists. We see the same phenomenon in US and Russian prisons: inmates must belong to a gang because only within the relative safety of group protection can any individual hope to survive given the high levels of violence within such institutions.

The cycle of self-perpetuating violence can be diminished when "justice" is substituted for revenge and a theoretically impartial third party can be relied upon to pursue and punish transgressors. Hence we see the evolution of tribal elder "courts" that sit in judgement on questions of tribe behavior. Later we see "the King's law" enforced by the ruler's functionaries across larger populations. In all such cases and even to our present day such regulatory entities are imperfect and not entirely effectual; nevertheless they enable a huge reduction in social violence simply because social norms tend to discourage individual action. It isn't usual in developed nations, for example, for a victim of assault to seek revenge upon their assailant. In the vast majority of cases the victim's primary concern is to involve the police so they can pursue the assailant on the victim's behalf.

Very few people in the West today take direct action against those who harm us, so deeply have we internalized the relevant social *moeurs* and so forcefully do the laws in developed nations punish anyone with the temerity to attempt to defend themselves or their families. This latter point in fact shows how poorly-considered laws can act against social justice when they are formulated by people lacking in the necessary domain expertise. In the UK, for example, the notion of "proportionate resistance" governs self-defense. In this wonderfully naïve theory the victim must magically predetermine precisely how much force the assailant will use and counter the assault with only the exact same amount of force. By this definition self-defense becomes a never-ending ballet in which the victim must foresee the assailant's every move and only counter it with equivalent force. If the victim successfully ends the assault, by definition they've used excessive force and are now guilty of a crime themselves. Such foolishness can only be precluded once we have a society in which intellectually competent people with relevant domain expertise are the only ones permitted to suggest and vote upon public policy and create laws.
Though most forms of justice in modern societies still leave a great deal to be desired, even a very imperfect form of abstracted justice is superior to a state in which families and clans band together for protection and thereby create an all-against-all system of interconnected feuds that can endure for generations.

Both the abstraction of wealth and the presence of independent third parties to establish and administer justice require sophisticated societies based on a generally accepted set of laws and customs and possessing mechanisms for the enforcement of such laws whenever necessary.

It can be argued that the illusion of these conditions being present must often compensate for their absence in reality. But there is more to the picture than this. We evolved within the context of social groups where behaviors and consequences are in general explicit. We know from the study of other social primates that the presence of older "authority figure" males confers stability; through various means including unconscious hormonal changes older males suppress the tendencies of juvenile males towards unruly behavior. In the absence of older male "authority figures" juvenile males tend to engage in more fights and attempt more rapes of females than would otherwise occur.

This is why modern innovations such as police officers patrolling in automobiles instead of following the old fashioned routine of "feet on the beat" are far less effective at inhibiting bad behavior by adolescents and young adults. Although the thrill of being able to race to a crime scene is doubtless gratifying and although the theoretical mobility afforded by automobiles is
superior to that afforded by foot or bicycle, the fact is that the psychological aspects of on-the-ground policing have been largely ignored in many developed countries since the end of World War II.

As many children grow up in homes lacking a father-figure, the police officer becomes a substitute in terms of being a strong male whose presence deters young males from excess; but an anonymous individual driving around in a car cannot perform this role. The consequence is that in a many places a significant amount of low-level violence and vandalism exists simply because there are no older male authority figures to provide a dampening effect. Any social policy developed in future needs to take into account our basic primate needs as much as any economic argument about efficiency. There are however issues we need to face when considering hardwired behavior, one of which is the problem of gender bias. If male authority figures are truly required to keep adolescent males in check this implies that female police officers should be tasked with other duties, for example detective work or surveillance, where gender is largely irrelevant. Today Political Correctness precludes any such notions and so no empirical tests can be made of the proposition and no lessons can be learned. One day, however, in order to achieve more equitable societies we will need to cast off lazy thinking and simple tropes in order to determine what actually works in the real world.

Moving on from the importance of securing safety and property we can now look at opportunity. Whenever opportunity is restricted to some hereditary caste, society as a whole suffers. This is for the same reason that kings are a sub-optimal solution to governance: the offspring of the talented are more likely than not to lack talent themselves and therefore be incompetent when placed in positions of influence merely because they are members of the lucky sperm club.

Although those fortunate enough to enjoy undeserved privilege may for a time luxuriate in the spoils, quite often they ultimately pay a very high penalty. The French and Russian revolutions are examples of how entire social strata may be eliminated within a brief period of time. The radical thinning-out of British aristocracy that occurred in World War One was also an unintended consequence of privilege. The young subalterns advancing across no-man's land with swagger-sticks clasped optimistically in their hands suffered an attrition rate far higher than that of the "other ranks" because they were required to lead from the front and thus be the first to receive enemy bullets. Today, although it's sadly unlikely that the Trump family will fall to the guillotine or the firing squad, we are seeing memes such as "eat the rich" which express the same general dissatisfaction with inept creatures who occupy positions of privilege merely because their parents created or acquired wealth many years ago. Who knows where such dissatisfaction will finally lead?

A hereditary caste system meanwhile means that society loses the potential gains that could have been realized if others, who were not fortunate enough to have been born into a particular caste or craft guild, could have found ways to utilize their natural aptitudes and interests. Few contributions to the wellbeing of mankind have been made by what so aptly used to be termed "the idle rich" while so many contributions have been made by those less privileged, despite the fact that they were striving against uneven odds. We cannot know what additional contributions might have been made by those who could never secure sufficient time and resources for study, reflection, and creation. The loss is incalculable and we have all missed out in ways we can never know.

Just as hereditary privilege is a deadweight on society, so too when craft guilds are rigorously enforced we end up with stifling conformity and lack of innovation. All the major advances in medicine over the last century have been made not by doctors (who belong to what is in essence a rigid craft guild) but by scientists and engineers. Conversely there have been no meaningful advances in law because lawyers have retained their craft guild privileges and thus no innovation can occur despite the fact that our societies are greatly over-burdened by archaic legal systems that serve only those who work within them while inflicting huge harm on society as a whole.

Any craft guild will tend over time to promote its own interests over those of society as a whole. Thus teachers' unions promote policies that make life easier for their members at the expense of the children whose education is supposedly paramount. Everywhere we see teachers' unions rejecting studies that show how pedagogy may be improved, how timetables could be made more effective, and how poorly performing teachers should be sanctioned while high performing colleague should reap rewards. The same behavior is seen wherever a craft guild mentality predominates, and it's always detrimental to society as a whole.

In an attempt to counter the inevitable proclivities of self-serving craft guilds, some governments have attempted to utilize market forces. Observing that for-profit corporations cannot indulge in the same degree of inefficiency and customer-hostile behavior as government-run organizations, several countries have concluded that pay-to-play in the educational realm is the way to counter the regressive tendencies of teachers' unions. The problem is that reliance on market forces assumes customers who can afford to pay for the goods on offer. Any cash-based system will inevitably discriminate against those from poorer backgrounds because they lack the financial insulation enjoyed by children born to better-off parents. So once again society as a whole loses out because a significant number of individuals will conclude that they cannot afford the financial risk of buying a university education, or paying for adequate dentistry, or going to see a doctor about a developing medical issue.

A rational system of resource allocation must be domain-appropriate. With education, it's essential to recognize that everyone in society benefits from all children having the chance of a good education. Likewise everyone benefits if each person is able to access adequate medical care in conjunction with other policies that promote good lifestyle choices and penalize poor choices. Too many governments fail to understand that market forces can only work in a system in which money or a proxy is able to send meaningful signals and producers are able to respond to such signals. Failing this, so-called market forces are not helpful but deeply harmful because they are not forces within a functioning market at all but merely instruments of exclusion. The British in particular have traveled a very long way down entirely the wrong road because this simple intellectual distinction was never made.

Taking our argument a little further, if government should provide free education out of general tax revenues it is clear that society has an interest in ensuring that education is both appropriate and well-delivered. The worst of all possible outcomes is seen in the USA where education is outrageously expensive yet far too many young people pursue degrees that have no utility. Neither society nor the individual gains from a degree in Movie Studies or when forty thousand graduates with Fine Arts degrees pursue four actual job openings. While it is always dangerous to attempt to predict precisely which skills will be valuable twenty years hence it is apparent that we really do need more engineers, dentists, plumbers, physicists, chemists, doctors, electricians and computer programmers and far fewer specialists in History of Art, Sociology, and Classical Greek, not to mention Gender Studies and Journalism.

Furthermore the US attachment to "general education" means that far too many students drop out before completing their degrees because they have to wade through many irrelevant classes before being able to attend the courses they actually want to pursue. Lest anyone jump to the defense of an attempt to create "well-rounded individuals" we can observe simply that US citizens are not notably more informed, worldly, and well-rounded than their European counterparts who study only their chosen subject and complete their tertiary education in a far shorter time and at far less expense.

It is reasonable for society to ensure that more places are available for those pursuing education that has a high utility and that fewer places are available for those pursuing education that has less utility. While Zoe may lament the fact that the decisions of a bourgeois society prevent her from being subsidized for several years in order to study Radical Marxist-Feminist Hermeneutic Critiques of the Calculus as a Tool of the Patriarchy, her inability to do so is a coherent social choice that maximizes social utility and minimizes Zoe's probability of being unemployable throughout the course of her life.

Arguing that utility isn't the only measure of value is pointless for in the end education must be paid for and there is a finite amount of money and therefore either price or a limit on course numbers must ultimately restrict demand. Jake may be passionate about fifteenth-century French choral music but if there are already far more graduates in this subject than potential jobs, Jake will after graduating end up in a low-paid service economy job that will neither satisfy him nor repay society's investment in his education.

Price is a woefully inefficient method for limiting access to education because it increases social divisions but does not address the question of utility; therefore limitation of courses is the only feasible mechanism by means of which to ensure that overall economic and individual efficacy are maximized. We should not live in a world where Suzanne can spend a pleasant four years studying for a degree that will leave her with few employment prospects simply because her parents are wealthy, while society as a whole continues to suffer a shortage of skilled workers. Education policy is a key component of any efficient and egalitarian society and must be structured to promote the values that ensure society is best placed to provide its citizens with rewarding work and also best placed to cope with the inevitable shocks and disruptions that are consequent upon innovation and a global economy.

A voucher system whereby students redeem their vouchers at the institution of their choice so that the institution then exchanges vouchers for government reimbursement enables market signaling without the concomitant distortions wrought by classes-for-cash. Each individual receives a certain number of vouchers sufficient for education and applies them as they see fit, within the constraints resulting from overall social requirements. Educational establishments that do a poor job of delivering value will see a reduction in numbers of students while those that perform well will see an increase in student numbers. In this way poor establishments are encouraged to self-correct or face oblivion while high performing establishments act as incubators of best practice and can be copied so that over time the average standard rises across the nation, which is clearly in the nation's best interest. It also means innovation can occur, as establishments attempt to improve their outcomes by evidence-based trial-and-error.

We must also become far more conscious than we are today that education is not a point-event but a lifelong process. A significant reduction in individual economic disruption can be achieved when citizens are life-long learners always acquiring new skills. Our present model of twelve years or so of primary and secondary education plus a few years of apprenticeship or undergraduate and post-graduate education followed by the rest of one's life with little or no additional formal education is clearly inadequate for today's rapidly-changing world. Thus pertinent education free at the point of delivery throughout one's life is an essential requirement for any modern society that wishes to maximize both individual and national utility and thereby enable the greatest level of professional career growth and personal satisfaction as well as the highest feasible level of GDP and subsequent revenues from taxation.

Greater freedom of choice is one of the primary differences between collectivist-style societies such as Mao's China and Stalin's USSR and more open societies such as those in the West. Freedom of choice is far more than a luxury or an indulgence for without freedom of choice there can be no economic efficiency. Without economic efficiency (in the broadest sense, here to mean the ability of individuals to enter into occupations for which they are best suited by temperament and aptitude) we cannot have meaningful freedom of individual choice. The two are mutually supportive.

For all that we can rightly bemoan the ephemeral trivia generated by Western consumer societies, we must recognize that our societies are more efficient and more conducive to individual freedom than the economies of closed societies where production and often occupation is dictated in a top-down manner. Our supermarket shelves are not typically bereft of food products and of such basic hygiene items as toilet paper and tampons. In contrast, in the ultimate command-economy of North Korea, millions of citizens regularly face acute starvation and are frequently reduced to eating mud and grass. In the command economy of the USSR people queued for hours without any guarantee that there would be anything left by the time they reached the head of the queue, nor that if there was indeed something left that it would be worth purchasing. And their work was rarely rewarding, being too often quite obviously purposeless and intended merely to hit nonsensical production quotas for things that nobody wanted.

This is why "green" and old-style socialist policies predicating top-down control of production are inevitably doomed to create massive economic inefficiency, a reduction of personal freedom of choice and action, and ultimately result in economic failure. While it appeals to the psychology of certain types of people to wish to restrict the choices of others, this is not a valid basis for a fair or efficient society.

We need to remember that each of us, driven by basic primate behaviors, is seeking to obtain advantage over others. Just because someone proclaims loudly that they want to restrict the freedom of others "for the good of the planet" or "for the general good" doesn't make it necessarily true. Nor does it mean that the effects of the proposed policies will achieve what is being claimed for them. We should always ask, *cui bono*? The strong may strive for dominance with their fists while the physically weak or fearful may strive for dominance using concepts and words. But regardless of what weapon is chosen, they are all deployed toward the same end: personal advantage.

Our "social warriors" aren't necessarily cynically attempting to achieve personal gain at the expense of others. Sometimes, true enough, they are but more often however people genuinely believe they are acting for the general good. We humans are very poor judges of our own true motivations. This is why yesterday's pipe-smoking woolen sweater wearing socialists are so often today's pipe-smoking woolen sweater wearing greens. The overt rationale may have changed but the underlying impulse remains the same: to tell other people what they can't have.

Let's face it: there's no better feeling than being able to tell someone else they can't have what they want because we're a better judge of what's right and good than they are.

As we consider all aspects of self-governance and the subsequent details of social policy it's essential we're always aware that things are rarely quite as they are made to seem. Even when a policy is genuinely formulated with good intentions, our basic intellectual limitations mean that it will often yield quite undesirable consequences when put into practice. Caution and skepticism are required when evaluating potential policy proposals. We must always ask: "how shall we evaluate the real-world outcomes?"

Improving the Improvements

The issue of evaluating proposals and trying to determine probable real-world outcomes is of course highly relevant to the various proposals that appear throughout this book. The intention is that the general population may benefit and that individual gaming of whatever system emerges will be very difficult. But every concept has flaws and empirically-based continuous adjustments are the only way to stay ahead of those who would seek to exploit systemic weaknesses in the pursuit of personal gain.

In addition it may seem strange to some readers that in the field of education just a few pages ago we proposed to restrict the number of available places for certain subjects, yet we also note that top-down command-and-control approaches are generally harmful. Surely these positions are incompatible?

In fact there is a substantial difference between the two topics and it's worth exploring for a few moments to understand why. With regards to education, society is paying through taxation. Unlimited choice ultimately means unlimited taxation which is of course unsupportable. For the production of material outputs, the market is best placed to send signals of desirability to private profit-driven corporations; the whims of bureaucrats in this sector of the economy are an extremely poor alternative. The problem for education is that its "goods and services" provide a very long-term return for society as a whole. The transient satisfaction of acquiring the latest consumer electronic device is in no way comparable to acquiring an education that will hopefully be the foundation of a productive and satisfying life.

Whereas markets are very good at responding to short-term signals they're notoriously poor at delivering good outcomes over longer time horizons. Were this not so we wouldn't presently be struggling with climate change, over-exploitation of natural resources, and the flood of misinformation shaping people's beliefs.

So different mechanisms are required in order to minimize unintended harm and increase intended good. If consumers want fish at the lowest possible price and this results in denuding the oceans of life governments can rightly step in because the preservation of global ecosystems is of much greater long-term importance than short-term corporate profits and today's low price for fish. We have to factor in the time dimension and give it its proper weight. This is something we humans are notoriously bad at because for almost all of our evolutionary history merely surviving until tomorrow was the greatest challenge we ever faced. Since the development of technology and the agricultural revolution we've consistently over-exploited every resource we can lay hands on because our tiny primate brains have no capacity to look beyond tomorrow morning. Therefore any system of government we adopt needs to compensate for our hardwired inability to think ahead. Often this will create conflict between people's desire for short-term gain and the overall needs of the world on an ongoing basis.

To understand how we may begin to reconcile these opposing forces we need to look at the basic operation of any economy.

Economies need two key factors in order to be reasonably efficient. The first is that money or its equivalent such as vouchers must be free to act as a signaling mechanism. The second is that governments must intervene as required (a) to prevent the emergence of cartels and monopolies, and (b) mitigate the harmful effects of short-term profit chasing.

In an open market economy mitigation is required because companies will always seek to offload costs onto society in order to maximize their profits. Without strict laws and suitable punishments, companies will further their own interests by imposing enormous costs on society. Examples of such costs include foul air, poisoned water, unsustainable depletion of natural resources, and the production and distribution of products that are intrinsically harmful. Today our laws and punishments are aimed at the abstraction of the corporation, while decisions and actions are undertaken by human beings. The 2008 financial crisis was caused by individuals seeking to maximize their personal wealth but the resultant fines were charged against the corporations which simply passed on these costs to shareholders and customers. No meaningful change of behavior resulted simply because no actual people were held accountable aside from a tiny number of low-ranking individuals who were thrown to the wolves in order to create the illusion of punishment.

Future systems of government must be far more cognizant of the need to ensure individuals feel they can be held accountable, otherwise such individuals will rightly understand that they can escape the consequences of their actions and therefore won't need to change their behaviors even when these behaviors can devastate entire economies or ecosystems.

It follows from our discussion about efficiency that we should be constrained by laws that seek to prevent us from harming others but otherwise we should in general be free to live our lives as we see fit. If Mary chooses to be a vegan and Peter chooses to consume fish and meat, these are personal choices and neither harms the other by following their preferences provided that foods are sourced sustainably and ethically. Similarly if Naomi wishes to cycle to work but Bob prefers to jog, each benefits and no costs are imposed on those around them. Tanya and Derek have decided that they don't want offspring, but Susan and Arthur have decided that they are prepared to work longer hours in order to be able to afford to raise three children. The list of such examples is endless and the personal satisfaction derived is immense. Conversely Peter isn't allowed to smoke his pipe in the office because servicing his addiction creates harmful pollutants that damage the health of his non-smoking co-workers. Jenna can't be allowed to commute on her two-stroke-powered skateboard because the pollution it emits harms the environment. And Igor shouldn't be able to shoot one of the last snow leopards merely because he's rich enough to charter a helicopter gunship.

At a larger scale this means the fishing industry can't be permitted to over-fish the oceans and employ methods that devastate entire ecosystems, as is the case today with deep-sea trawling. It means that we must step in to outlaw products resulting from the imposition of massive ecological harm such as anything to do with coconuts (which presently Western consumers incorrectly believe can confer various health benefits), animal products, and the like. Although no single country can successfully address this global problem we must begin somewhere and a well-governed nation is our best chance to begin coherently. Others may, in time, follow.

Returning to the original question, what does all this have to do with education? Simply put, society has a large long-term interest in education being appropriate for its long-term needs. While bureaucrats will always be hopeless at "picking winners" there is a lot of empirical data that shows society as a whole becomes enriched when we focus educational resources on certain types of knowledge. Science outweighs so-called "social science" (which is neither truly social nor in any way scientific) by enormous margins. Of course we don't wish for, nor could we have, a society comprised entirely of engineers, physicists, and mathematicians. Most people lack the cognitive abilities necessary to thrive in such domains. But we clearly need more than we currently possess, and equally clearly we have a great deal more Art History, Sociology, and Media Studies graduates than will ever find jobs in these fields. Furthermore, a scientific education helps people to reason more adequately whereas studies based on empty assertions and transiently fashionable notions fail to expand adequately our intellectual capacities. This in turn means fewer citizens qualified to weigh in on important matters, and that's surely a huge loss for everyone concerned.

Equally society derives no benefit and often suffers significant harm from so-called "religious education" which is merely the promulgation of primitive mythologies. At best it is a waste of everyone's time; at worst it leads to madrassas that radicalize naïve youngsters who then go on to inflict great harm on those around them.

So a more adequately governed society would require a more adequate approach to education. Facts and reasoning would predominate over empty assertions and folk beliefs. This in turn would slowly help promote a more thoughtful and informed population which in turn could make more adequate decisions both on an individual basis and at larger scales. Today we abdicate self-improvement and expect *them* to make adequate choices on our behalf. We infantilize ourselves and complain when mommy and daddy government doesn't give us the free ice-cream we believe we deserve. Such self-indulgent intellectual indolence is both morally and practically insupportable. We need to start taking individual responsibility for becoming more adequate citizens because if we don't, we surely can't expect more adequate governance to appear over the horizon as if by magic.

Governance ultimately comprises a series of choices, beginning with the individual and proceeding outward through family, social groups, and ultimately to nations and collections of nations.

The same fundamental principles operate across all sizes of social group which is why we may in many cases begin with individuals in order to elaborate general principles that can subsequently be expanded to encompass many or even all. When Celeste studies physics she acquires a habit of mind that will enable her to make far more rational decisions about all aspects of her life. A community of Celestes collectively will make more rational decisions about matters that impact us all.

Today many of the world's most successful people are merely those who can fool others into believing them. The vast majority of business leaders and politicians are little more than plausible performers whose actual capabilities are woefully short of what is required. People talk themselves into positions of power and then flounder until the next plausible rogue supplants them. By developing an education system that emphasizes thinking and competence we're far more likely to judge by results than by bluster. This will, over time, help to create a more egalitarian society in which individual contributions are properly appreciated. A diligent brick-layer is far more valuable than a blustering incompetent money-losing casino owner and television performer manqué.

An egalitarian society focused on real accomplishments and performance also will help mitigate our universal human tendency to hark back to an imaginary golden age, so we can be more open to innovation and stop looking backward for yesterday's "solutions" to today's problems. For as long as we humans have been able to record our thoughts we've been lamenting the loss of a past that is far better than our present degenerate condition. It's unhelpful that we should be nostalgic for a past that exists only in our imaginations and which has been carefully cleared of all recollection that would militate against such a rose-tinted view but we all are guilty of it. Such false rearward-looking leads inevitably to regressive attitudes and disastrous policies. Much of today's populism/nationalism is little more than a collective desire to hide under the bed and pretend that magically yesterday was so much better than today.

We need to build in, as much as possible, attitudes and structures that limit our ability to deceive ourselves about what came before. As long as we are mourning an imaginary past in which we were all more decent and safer than we are today we are less open to constructive change that will preserve the present and improve the future. An egalitarian society removes many of the mental props that support nostalgia. Without an aristocracy, for example, we can't pretend there was a time when "they" knew what was good for us all, or when "they" manifested our virtues. Without yearning for a racist past we can't pretend that things were better when "they knew their place." When we remember the past accurately we will be less likely to blame "them over there" for our present discontents. And therefore we will be less prone to being manipulated by those who wish, by controlling our notions of the past, to control the way we think of the present.

Today's crop of demagogues have shown clearly how our nostalgia makes us feel that the past was a better, safer, happier place and therefore something must have gone wrong for the present to be so disappointing in comparison. We are then impelled by our discontent to seek "solutions" to what are essentially problems that exist only in our imaginations.

In recent years we have seen the British voting for economic and social backwardness via Brexit, Hungary taking several steps back towards totalitarianism, Russia indulging a kleptomaniac regime in the name of "the Slavic destiny," Poland returning to a form of right-wing theocracy, Turkey heading back to a medieval theological notion of the State, and the USA voting for an intellectually stunted orange buffoon unfit to run even a hot-dog stall merely because he promised uneducated obese white people that a return to the 1950s was possible.

It is clear therefore that future systems of governance must take into account our tendency toward nostalgia and devise ways to minimize the harm that can result. Removing representatives is one important step; regulating media to minimize the transmission of lies and propaganda is another. Entertainment, with its faux-realistic depictions of the past in which people miraculously lack the actual skin diseases, bad teeth, crooked backs, and various other deficiency-related ailments of the past, also has a surprisingly large role to play.

If we're going to indulge in costume dramas, dramatists must have a responsibility to portray accurately the times. Where, for example, in all the British telenovelas about the Victorian age do we see tiny children being forced up narrow chimneys, the children missing hands and arms because of industrial accidents, the twisted victims of polio and rickets, and the pockmarked beggars dying of starvation in the streets while "polite society" carefully steps around them? Where in such telenovelas do we see people dying of bacterial infections, seeping with pus from weeping cancerous growths, or succumbing to typhoid, measles, whooping-cough, mumps, and a thousand other diseases that today we've practically vanquished? Where's all the childhood mortality? Where is the shit on the streets? Isn't it remarkable that the characters in such "historical" dramas have such wonderfully white and perfect teeth and clean hair and absolutely no body lice that require near-constant scratching?

There will be many changes required on the long road towards encouraging a more realistic appraisal of both past and present, of defeating long-held but unexamined ideas, and moving towards a society in which choices are more often based on fact than on fantasy. It's time for us to get started on the journey. And helping develop an educated and informed population is an essential first step.

Groups and Figureheads

There are few pleasures more beguiling than to solve the problems of the world by dreaming up wonderful solutions that would be splendid if only people were slightly different from how we actually are. This type of wishful thinking can manifest in any field of human endeavor, sometimes with risible consequences. British soldiers from the 1970s will recall the Blowpipe man-portable air-defense system that would have worked splendidly if only human beings had three arms and two heads. Marxist economics would work wonderfully if only natural selection didn't favor self-interest.

If we want to avoid having our own Blowpipe or Soviet experiences we need to accept fundamental behavioral hardwiring and work within its constraints.

We're primates. We evolved to cope with far simpler environments than pertain today. In a very real sense we're cave-people struggling to exist in a world of technological marvels and global complexity that is quite beyond the capacity of most people to understand. And we're not going to abandon our deepest instincts and drives just because there's a dysfunctional mismatch between our feelings and the reality around us. We may be asleep at the wheel but as long as we can stroke our smartphones we'll continue to believe we're doing a great job.

One key aspect of our behavioral repertoire is our persistent need for a leader. All of our organizations are hierarchical. Where alternatives have been tried they have failed abysmally. Why is this?

Under the conditions that have pertained throughout our evolutionary history, decision-making and action are achieved more rapidly and coherently under leadership of a single person than under any form of conglomerate. Imagine a tribe of people living fifty thousand years ago who, when facing invasion by another tribe, attempted collective decision-making. Chances are the invading tribe would have slaughtered everyone before consensus was reached. In consequence of this we have an evolved instinct to play follow-the-leader because that enables rapid decision-making. This instinct is much more powerful than our slender and intermittent attempts at reason.

We need a leader but in modern democracies we place an unrealistic burden of expectation upon him (or, more rarely, her) that inevitably cannot be met and so we're disappointed. If only we had a better leader, all would be well!

Our monkey brains need the leader to provide the right answers and give us the right guidance. The illusion of adequacy is difficult to maintain in a representative democracy but much easier to establish and maintain in a tyranny. In totalitarian regimes the Great Leader is always ubiquitous but also distant. We can project our fantasies onto him without hindrance. When the realities of life are in fact dire we blame the intermediaries. "If only the Great Leader knew, then he'd fix things. But of course he's so busy, and they don't let him know what's going on down here."

But in the West it's all too easy to notice when the leader is failing to live up to our expectations; many journalists and pundits make their livings exclusively from pointing out every defect and shortfall, real or imagined. In repressive regimes it is possible for the leader to manipulate information and punish potential nay-sayers so as to reduce or eliminate the gap between reality and wished-for fantasy. In more open societies however the gap results in disillusionment which is why so many people today have largely given up on "politics as usual" and why in the commercial sphere some rightly question the enormous rewards given to CEOs who are at best mediocre. As a result the interval between adulation and disillusionment has shrunk dramatically over the last fifty years, creating ever-more-rapid turnover among both politicians and CEOs.

The problem is that removing one leader and substituting the next does nothing to solve the systemic problems of leadership in a complex and rapidly-changing world. Organizations that tamper with hierarchy generally devolve into ineffectual rule-by-committee in which the key principle is "don't rock the boat." Many large corporations become moribund and eventually destroy enough shareholder value that they either go bankrupt or are acquired and restructured by outsiders. This is not, however, an option for a national government, some version of which can limp on for decades after becoming hopelessly inadequate. Changes of stewardship under one Party or another make very little difference, which is why we have witnessed systemic political decline of the political Party into complete irrelevance.

There are two strands to the issue of leadership. One is the need for rapid and unambiguous decision-making which hitherto has required the centralization of power. This strand we have addressed earlier with the notion of pre-determined decisions and policies that will be automatically executed upon the relevant trigger event. The other strand we must now consider is our primal need for a visible group "leader" to whom we can all look up and in whom we can place our unrealistic hopes and expectations.

Or to put it another way, just as small children need a favorite cuddly toy in which they can repose their instincts for affection and need for love, we all need a Great Helmsperson on the bridge of the Ship of State to satisfy our hardwired need for a group leader in whom we can repose our trust and hopes.

Unless we adequately satisfy this primitive need, no intellectual superstructure no matter how elegant or apparently suitable will long survive an encounter with the real world. We're a group species, therefore we need a leader who can personify our hopes, aspirations, dreams, and desires. Today pop-stars and presidents are our surrogate "leaders" and sports teams and various issue-oriented organizations are our surrogate groups. Yet none really suffice. We still yearn for the "wise leader" who, over decades, can provide a comforting continuity within which we can frame our lives.

Several European countries have by virtue of their origins in the era of early aristocracy inherited figureheads called "royalty." Such individuals have evolved to embody vague but emotionally important notions of nationhood, probity, and continuity. At the same time they have no meaningful political power and thus cannot disappoint through making poor decisions or vacillating during times of crisis. Although the cost of having a queen is the continuation of a hereditary structure that is intrinsically non-egalitarian and regressive, the benefit is that the people get a long-term figurehead in whom they can invest their emotions while avoiding the problems resulting from the figurehead possessing actual political power and thus being likely to make huge mistakes on an embarrassingly regular basis.

For a more egalitarian age we may want to replace a queen with an elected Head of State whose tenure is for life. We can even imagine that such a Head of State would come from the pool of citizens who have contributed to the public good through charitable works or other altruistic acts.

Unfortunately our experience of appointed Presidents in countries like Germany, Italy, and Israel has not been entirely satisfactory. One reason is that such Presidents do retain some political role within the Constitution; another is that little intentional symbolic commingling of person with nation has thus far been attempted. Most Presidents are merely former politicians, which hardly qualifies anyone to be a reliable repository of hopes and illusions. With sufficient study it may be possible to identify the optimal characteristics of a national figurehead so that we can get better at fabricating this necessary position. If we don't it's a safe bet that a significant percentage of the population will look for alternatives, often sporting funny little moustaches, who are very likely to be harmful to social stability.

In addition to our hardwired need for a leader we also have a profound need to feel part of at least one substantial and long-lasting group. So we have to meet this need for identity through group membership in the most benign ways possible.

It is probable, *pace* the requirement for a suitable figurehead, that emotionally satisfying group structures must also be divorced from any significant real-world actions. Ideally, groups will have aims that aim to promote positive interactions with other similar groups. Yet this latter characteristic will tend to be very difficult to sustain because human psychology will always tend towards hostility, or at the very least covert antagonism, towards other groups. During our evolutionary history the balance between intra-group cooperation and intra-group hostility was always very delicate.

The violence that accompanied most soccer matches in the UK during the 1970s and the atavistic chanting of Trump supporters in recent years show us how easily we become deeply identified with a group and consequently perform all sorts of absurd acts that serve no rational purpose whatsoever. Even when there is no outward antagonism, rational cooperation between groups is a rare phenomenon.

A simple example will serve to illustrate how even the most apparently benign groups can end up in conflict with each other. Let's imagine two charitable organizations, each of which prides itself on famine relief. Let's call these organizations Alpha and Beta and the country currently experiencing famine is Zenovia.

Both Alpha and Beta race to establish their presence in Zenovia, motivated by a genuine desire to help the people there. Although both want to help the starving people of Zenovia, they establish separate operating bases and liaise separately with Zenovia's various governmental institutions. Alpha and Beta bid against each other for assets like trucks that will be used to transport food to starving people, thus increasing the profit of the truck companies but not increasing the amount of food that ultimately will be distributed to hungry Zenovians. They will also compete in bidding for food supplies, thus increasing the profits of middle-men but not increasing the total amount of food available for famine relief. Because Alpha and Beta both depend on donations from the public, they must also compete for media exposure. So regardless of any altruistic feelings individuals working for the two organizations may have, the reality is a zero-sum competition.

This example, anonymized to spare the blushes of two well-known real-world organizations, is drawn from the most well-meaning and most benign sort of organization. It's not difficult to imagine far more unpleasant outcomes arising from a clash between groups promoting opposing values on matters of race, sexual preference, social hierarchy, type of employment, national identity, and so on.

Conflict with others is built in to the very concept of group identity. So we need to engineer groups in order to minimize the potential for destructive conflict.

What characteristics should a group have in order to be a suitable mechanism for providing psychological succor?

- The group must have no entrance requirement; this permits anyone to become a member and dilutes the tendency of the group to acquire discriminatory tendencies arising out of any accidental homogeneity among the original group members.

- The group should have persistence, ideally over a generation. Without persistence the group cannot provide psychological reassurance to its members.

- The group must have a leader who has ceremonial powers but no practical authority.

This kind of social engineering may not seem a very realistic idea but wherever we look we see very successful intentionally constructed groups. In developed societies young men no longer form raiding parties that seek out other similar groups of young men in order to engage in violent conflict for the "honor" of the tribe. Instead we have ritualized fighting in the form of soccer, American football (along with its requisite young females cheering on their young warriors), and all manner of other team sports. Today most people are spectators and associate with the group vicariously, but all sports began life as somewhat violent participatory pursuits that gradually became more and more benign substitutes for violent encounters.

Some countries have had relatively recent experience of intentionally constructed groups, very often designed to channel the energies of young people. In the mid-twentieth century Germany had the Hitler Youth and for nearly seventy years the USSR had its Pioneers. The West had Boy Scouts and Girl Guides to fulfill much the same purpose. For the most part these groups have been very successful in capturing the imagination and devotion of a significant portion of the population, which indicates that it is not a particularly difficult thing to construct such groups and then gain acceptance for them in a relatively short period of time.

We can imagine that a certain amount of experimentation and learning from experience will be required in order to arrive at a suitable arrangement of stable groups that provide a suitable sense of affiliation and at the same time are essentially harmless.

Few groups can persist over extended periods of time without the original ethos deteriorating, so groups may have to be dissolved through some agreed mechanism and new groups formed that can channel the natural enthusiasm of youth for pastures new. In all probability the duration of the group is likely to coincide with the average life-span of its members from age twenty or so until death so as to maintain continuity for current members.

Much of our civilization is built upon the channeling of raw primate impulse into more positive courses. For the most part our groups have evolved over time by trial and error and remain very imperfect because they have evolved without our being aware of our most basic hardwired impulses. We can now aspire to design such groups more adequately, especially if we accept the fact that such attempts will always be a work in progress where we learn from the past in order to fashion better in the future. If we accept that it is entirely moral to encourage young men to play in or support soccer teams instead of attacking each other with sticks and knives, we can agree that conscious creation and management of groups is a valid mechanism for achieving a socially desirable outcome. Provided that we can ensure group stability over a suitable amount of time our intentional groups can give us the sense of meaning and community that we need in our lives and which today for all too many people is lacking.

If we consider for a moment the contemporary phenomenon of Islamic terrorism we see that most of those eager to join ISIS and other similar death cults were not driven by religious belief. Many, indeed, had little or no grasp of the religion they professed to follow. They were driven primarily by the need to find meaning in their lives. They affiliated with groups that appeared to have such a clear purpose that even the most intellectually under-developed mind could grasp it. Recruits thereby acquired a greater sense of self than was otherwise possible, even if ultimately it resulted in the loss of their lives. From this type of behavior we can deduce how important it is for us to feel part of a group and therefore how important it is that we understand and incorporate this requirement into any future system of governance. Unless people are relatively satisfied, adequate governance is highly unlikely to be sustained.

Evolve or Die

It's easy to note the many ways in which representative democracy has failed. It's easy to be angry at the unfairness and stupidity of everyday life, even when we ourselves are contributing to that unfairness and stupidity. Representative democracy stumbled into existence as a series of expedients intended to address once-important issues but never developed the internal mechanisms needed for it to evolve so as to be able to cope with contemporary problems. So today we have a very dysfunctional system of governance indeed.

In many of our current implementations of governance the wealthy and powerful essentially buy the political class in order to promote their own interests. Examples include tobacco and food and firearms companies lobbying for legislation that permits them to make profits at the expense of society as a whole, and industrial companies lobbying for legislation that permits them to avoid the full costs of generating pollution. Meanwhile billionaires are taxed on a smaller percentage of income than a typical middle-class worker. There are a great many other examples; the point is that our social system is sufficiently dysfunctional that it permits a tiny number of individuals to benefit at the expense of the great majority.

It's a lovely system if you're rich and powerful.

And that's one of the reasons why it's so easy to stoke the fires of popular discontent. Wealth disparity today is more or less at its historical norm but we've been deeply influenced by the atypical situation that existed between 1945 and 1995. During this period, unlike all other periods in history, the ordinary person's income and standard of living rose dramatically while the ultra-rich didn't experience anything like a similar rise. In some countries, new tax rules meant inherited wealth no longer assured members of "the lucky sperm club" a lifetime of luxurious indolence. In the UK, for example, hundreds of stately homes and their adjunct estates were given to the National Trust when their inheritors couldn't afford to pay the inheritance taxes. But today in many countries the tax laws favor the rich. For example, capital gains on investments are taxed at a much lower rate than income. This is wonderful if you're rich, because you can make many investments. It's not so lovely if you're struggling to feed a family and keep a roof over your head while working three low-paid jobs in a desperate attempt to make ends meet.

Gross disparity of wealth creates two problems. The first, and actually minor, problem is that it makes the rest of us envious. It is, frankly, galling to see some well-groomed imbecile enjoying luxuries we will never be able to afford merely because his Daddy is rich. The more important problem is that, contrary to the ludicrous assertions of George Laffer, giving enormously wealthy people even more money does not "trickle down" into the rest of the economy. There are only so many estates, private jets, yachts, and over-priced sports cars a person can buy. There are only so many maids, butlers, and gardeners a person can employ. The rest of the money goes into investment portfolios that are rarely more than passive and thus do nothing to stimulate innovation and encourage widespread wealth creation.

Worst of all is the pilfering of wealth that is common in many Asian and in all African countries. Here there's not even the pretense of a tax regime; the powerful simply steal flagrantly and send the stolen cash in suitcases to their favorite Swiss banks. Capital that could have been directed towards productive uses is instead sequestered in the vaults of foreign banks, to be converted into French chateaux and London flats and spent on absurdly expensive wrist-watches, luxury cars, and liver-wrecking amounts of vintage champagne.

Furthermore, even when we're merely talking about the profits of large corporations, there's the problem of social cost. As we noted earlier, many legal products that are highly profitable also just happen to cause enormous harm. Cigarettes, alcohol, and junk food are three obvious examples. Sadly there are many, many more to be found. In the USA the NRA reliably blocks any attempt to prevent more than 30,000 annual gunshot deaths and an additional 100,000 annual gunshot injuries in order to protect fewer than 40,000 jobs. This is a sad example how readily we humans passively accept any *status quo* no matter how dysfunctional and frankly insane it may be.

Today the ordinary taxpayer subsidizes the multi-million dollar compensation packages of the executives running large corporations because taxpayers' money is used to compensate for the harm these corporations inflict on society. Whether it is lung cancer, diabetes, polluted waterways, or a dead child, the story is always the same: the corporations pocket the profits while society picks up the costs.

A similar story is emerging with the Internet. Although the Internet provides some modest benefits (the ability to binge-watch a TV series, or go to Wikipedia to assist with a research project) it also imposes massive costs: an echo-chamber for lies that poison civic society and enable absurd creatures to stumble incoherently into positions of power. There has never in all of human history been such a mechanism to spread lies among the ignorant and credulous. We are quite literally pouring junk into people's brains and then wondering why they get sick. But don't worry: this makes Google and Facebook and plenty of other large corporations very rich, so that's all right then.

What all this means for governance is that we've got to be able to take into account a great many external factors. There's little point creating a better system of governance if we just continue to accept economic and social distortions. This in turn means we have to understand that yesterday's problem and putative solution will rarely be relevant to tomorrow's important challenges. Our ability to identify problems must be as capable of evolving as any other aspect of our desired system of governance.

It's easy enough to imagine a carbon tax, regulations that enforce anti-pollution measures, and even the reform of taxation so as to minimize economic distortions. But we need to understand that pollution comes in many forms and today we need to grapple with infotainment pollution. What people believe strongly influences what people do. False beliefs therefore guarantee poor outcomes.

Let's look at the dynamics of the problem.

Every purveyor of infotainment is in a competition to grab eyeballs. The more eyeballs you can grab, the more valuable your ad slots become or the more you can charge for a subscription or the more you can justify your government subsidy. The most reliable way to grab eyeballs is to provide sensationalist content, the more outlandish the better. That's why even supposedly "serious" news organizations such as the BBC regularly feature items of zero importance. A lost cat being returned to its owner, a sports personality getting divorced, a suspect on the run – none of these things has any significance to society as a whole but are featured because they have "human interest." But this is just intellectual pandering. It's like feeding your child nothing but sweets because "children like sweets." Yes, they do. But we know that what people like and what they actually need in order to be healthy are often two very different things.

Likewise Facebook has a far greater economic gain from feeding ultra-right-wing nationalists more of their own propaganda than in attempting to correct their distorted world view. Because we humans are far more influenced by anecdote than by facts, and far more easily roused by emotional content than by intellectual discourse, it is a simple matter to exploit these predispositions in the pursuit of profit.

We need to move to balance costs against benefits. If something is true it can be published, but supporting facts and context must also be provided. This would protect the much-claimed but in fact rarely seen investigative journalism of the sort that uncovered the Watergate and Iran-Contra misdeeds, but prevent blustering morons from infecting the world with blatant lies. When facts are required by law, lies evaporate. And when context is required by law, our human mental limitations can to some degree be offset by relevant information.

For example, it is true that Flight UX888 crashed in Freilandia today and fifty-three people were killed; but it is also true that an individual's risk of being killed in such a crash is infinitesimally tiny compared to their likelihood of being injured or killed in an automobile collision. So if the news article states that worldwide today 53 people died in an aviation accident while approximately 4,100 people died in unremarked automobile accidents, what's your emotional take-away now?

As always, we must accept that our initial efforts must be subject to empirical assessment and improvement. No system can be perfect at the start and no system can remain adequate if it does not have the means whereby to improve itself continuously.

As we observed at the beginning of this book, we have come to expect continuous improvement in nearly all aspects of our lives. Open markets engender competition and competition spurs development. We cannot help but be struck by the similarities of an open market with evolution in the natural world. When ShinyTech Corp brings out a new product, GlitteryTech Inc strives quickly to out-innovate it and regain market share. When the springbok species evolves to run a little faster, the cheetah species evolves to run faster still.

The lesson for systems of governance is obvious: no matter how adequate today's solution, tomorrow people will find ways to subvert it. Our systems of governance must have inbuilt mechanisms that force them evolve. The difference between natural evolution and the evolution of systems of governance is that evolution is not teleological but the evolution of our systems of governance should be directed at an overall goal, which is to establish an ever-more humane society within which individuals have the greatest opportunity to thrive.

A thought experiment can demonstrate the equity of this goal. Let's imagine that we or our children will be born into our imaginary society without any ability to influence position in the social hierarchy. The most equitable society is that which offers the individual born into any particular stratum the greatest chance of thriving. And we use the word "thrive" in the widest sense: not mere material gain but also emotional and intellectual fulfilment. While a tyrant may be perfectly happy to sit at the apex of brutal exploitation it is unlikely they would choose their own society were they to occupy any potential place within it.

So in our notional system of enhanced governance we must keep a general goal in mind but recognize that we can't determine exactly how we'll pursue the goal. What we can do, however, is to ensure that our system of governance has built into its very fabric the mechanisms necessary to self-correct and evolve as individuals and groups seek to exploit opportunities at the expense of society as a whole. We humans are not going to change our hardwired behaviors so we have to design social mechanisms that constrain our seemingly endless capacity for self-harm.

This is how we now have a third-party system of justice that replaces the endless vendettas of less developed societies. We have sporting matches to engage the energy of young males rather than having tribal combat. These mechanisms have evolved over time, largely unconsciously, to solve persistent problems arising from evolved human behaviors. It is clear that as we learn more about ourselves and our limitations we will be in an increasingly better position to find ways to limit the harms done by behaviors that may have served us well fifty thousand years ago but are not so beneficial today.

It is obvious we can never rely on benevolent dictators or self-abnegating individuals to steer the ship of state for the benefit of all. Every one of us seeks individual advantage and the more power and influence we have the greater the distortions we can create. Society as a whole pays, but we as individuals gain disproportionately.

While Putin, Erdogan, Xi, Orban, Trump, and all the other inadequate personalities sitting on top of the heap doubtless persuade themselves they are acting "in the general good" the reality is the opposite. So we have to stop the emergence of more of the same, even after we've removed representatives from the equation. There will never be a shortage of wannabe tyrants looking to exploit the easily-fooled masses.

Self-evolving systems are essential if we're not going to fall back into tyranny after a short time. This is not a Utopian dream: to an astonishing extent we already have accomplished many of the basic goals of such a society. As Adam Smith noted, the great power of the open market is that individuals can seek their individual gain precisely by serving society at large. The farmer grows crops not out of benevolence but to gain money from selling them to people who wish to eat. The builder erects dwellings not out of altruism but rather to profit from those who wish to buy houses. The farmer and the builder can't exploit the hungry and homeless in an open market economy because if they set their prices too high then other farmers and builders will under-cut them and thus their income will be jeopardized. Each individual acts as a check on each other individual, so that few can easily exploit their fellows. It took society a long time to overcome the self-serving of craft guilds which intentionally restricted competition and supply in order to maintain high prices, but eventually some of the benefits of a market system were achieved. And unlike top-down government central planning, markets evolve to meet emerging circumstances. No government planner would have dreamed up the smartphone or the mass production techniques that have reduced the cost of nearly all consumer goods. These, and uncountable other benefits, emerged spontaneously from the evolutionary processes engendered by competitive markets.

Unfortunately, as we have seen, a relatively static system of governance is prey to those who discover ways to exploit its weaknesses. Our legal systems, our governments, our health care systems, and our systems of market and banking regulation have all become captured by the powerful and are thus largely dysfunctional now. We cannot hope to "repair" these systems because any meaningful attempts at reform are always blocked by the very powers that now control them to their own advantage. Once the shark has eaten the fish, you can't get the fish back again.

It is therefore clear that any improved systems of governance must have at their very core an ineradicable set of mechanisms that promote goal-oriented evolution by means of which we can always, just, outdistance the would-be predator.

What would such mechanisms look like? To begin with, we'd have to avoid fetishizing our Constitution. In the USA, as befits a highly religionist society, the Constitution has become a kind of sacred text instead of what it really is: a first draft work-in-progress template designed to be changed in order to better meet the needs of society as it changes through time. Instead, "textualists" claim that the Constitution is an infallible guide to matters undreamed of by the Founding Fathers. This intellectual incoherence is sadly what one would expect of those who also believe that the 3,000-year-old folk myths of a tribe of innumerate genocidal goat-herders are an infallible guide to living in the modern world. A system of governance based on a more intellectually adequate set of propositions could avoid falling into what we can safely call the USA Stunted Intellect Trap.

Next up, we'd need a method for detecting attempts to capture or game the system. While policy proposals need be presented anonymously it is nevertheless possible that a sub-set of qualified individuals could either by inference or direct collaboration know the source of a proposal and support (or reject) it on the basis of that individual's character, status, or other attribute. We can imagine, for example, a group of academic economists intentionally supporting a proposal made by an eminent colleague regardless of its intrinsic merit. The primary solution to this problem is scale: while at most a few dozen academics could band together in this way, it would be far more difficult to suborn hundreds or even thousands of non-academic qualified voters. Any attempt to do so should be detected and the proposal itself invalidated in consequence.

Similar collusion among parties with vested interests are likely to arise wherever we look, from a town counselor trying to organize support for her proposal to a group of bankers trying to ensure the passage of a policy that would favor their interests. In each case the primary solution is to ensure that there is a sufficiently large pool of non-affiliated qualified voters to nullify the effects of such attempts. Secondary methods of reducing such attempts to gain the system would have to include criminal penalties by means of which those individuals responsible would (a) be removed from their positions of influence, and (b) made to suffer appropriate penalties.

With the gradual development of artificial intelligence systems it will be possible to improve policy analysis so as to get better at projecting likely outcomes of new policies. This would help identify who would benefit and thereby enable other qualified voters to assess whether or not the new policy being proposed has merit beyond merely advancing the interests of a particular group of people.

We have never attempted to design a self-evolving system central to human social life and so our early efforts are bound to be limited, naïve, and crude. Yet if we do not start down this road we will not learn how to improve our ability to engineer such a system. And if our systems of governance cannot evolve in order to avoid being captured by special interests then no matter how rational and elegant the original conception, it will soon end up as dysfunctional as representative democracy. Learning how to build self-evolving systems is therefore an essential next task and it is to be hoped that progress can be made despite the economic and social disruptions that the current wave of populism/nationalism will inevitably inflict on every nation that succumbs to the mindlessness of the howling mob.

The Chains that Bind

When we consider the weight of vested interests commanding our systems of government and the intrinsic unwillingness of most of us to countenance major structural changes, we can't be optimistic that any significant improvement will occur in our lifetimes.

Professional politicians will hardly wish to engineer themselves out of their pleasant careers. The wealthy and powerful who purchase influence behind the scenes won't want to change the rules of a game over which they have significant control. The legions of bureaucrats whose employment depends on our present conception of affairs will naturally wish to continue in their jobs until comfortable retirement. Lobbyists depend on the people they so lucratively influence and the single-interest pressure groups that have learned so ably to manipulate both public perception and the mechanics of today's political system will likewise resist change. And we ourselves, especially when we are older, are loathe to alter a political structure that may be dysfunctional but has the sole merit of being familiar. And besides, haven't we all heard that democracy is better than any other form of government?

The fact is, although we like to blame particular politicians or Parties for the things we don't like, and hold the political class in low esteem because our systems of governance are so dysfunctional, we're the ones to blame. How many voters blithely accept whatever assertions spill out of the mouths of their favorite politicians and pundits? How few bother to undertake any meaningful research before casting their votes? We the people are the ultimate source of our own discontent. Unfortunately, even if we were to exercise appropriate diligence and reason, the system itself is so fundamentally flawed that no adequate outcomes are possible. Yet we continue to accept the system as though it were inconceivable that anything better could be engineered. At best we think that a change of Party or Leader will magically solve problems that are in fact systemic and unaffected by transient changes of personnel.

In addition to firmly entrenched resistance, no blueprint for an improved system of governance can emerge fully-formed and without flaw. The ideas sketched in this book merely point in a general direction; there is and can never be an infallible system prior to commencing. History teaches us quite clearly that when you try to build social systems upon supposedly infallible doctrines you create horrors, not heavens. Unfortunately people always want firm answers, not general directions for improvement. We are uncomfortable with ambiguity, which is why we invariably opt for whatever seems assured even when the assurances are implausible. It's impossible to imagine a majority of citizens in any nation voluntarily embracing a process rather than a glibly promised outcome.

Today we live as we have done for millennia: we accept assertion and rarely ask for evidence.
We need to change, to understand that a model that utilizes empiricism rather than assertion is the only way forward. We need systems that work by forming hypotheses, testing them, modifying them based on real-world outcomes, and iterating so we come ever-closer to our desired goals. This is how we get the benefits of smartphones and airplanes and all the other technological marvels we've come to expect as our due. It's long past time we applied the same basic principles to the problem of governance. Because today we're still treating governance as primitive tribes treated the weather:

something powered by gods whom the priests told us could be swayed by prayers and sacrifices.

We crave simplistic answers we can understand. But simplistic answers are forever inadequate to deal with complex problems. That's the fundamental human dilemma of our post-Enlightenment, post-industrial, age.

Some people object to the idea of putting competence in a central position, arguing that politics is about emotion as much as (or more than) thinking. This is a true statement, but it serves to indicate precisely why we need to make a radical change to our present way of organizing governance. Would we want to put emotion in first place in the cockpit of commercial airliners? We do have a few examples of what happens when airline procedures fail and emotional pilots take the yolk: they crash the aircraft and kill everyone on board. We have examples of what occurs when people get emotional behind the wheel of their car: it's called road rage. The idea that emotions evolved on the Savannah of Africa and the primordial forests of Eurasia are somehow suitable guides for dealing with the complexities of today's world is merely intellectual cowardice, a neo-Romantic fantasy that has no grounding in reality. In fact we desperately need more competence and far less misguided emotion. We need knowledge instead of ignorance, thought instead of impulse, and coherence instead of chaotic blundering.

The West is now faltering and there are no obvious candidates to pick up the mantle of progress; it is likely that a long period of tyrant-led barbarism will result. Just because most of us in the West are too lazy to acquaint ourselves with history doesn't mean that history won't ultimately roll over us and crush us.

The *annus horribilis* of 2016 seems to confirm that we are set on a course that will force us to recapitulate the stupidities and horrors of the mid twentieth century and thus apparently confirm Santayana's dictum that "those who cannot learn from history are doomed to repeat it." Worse, we may be about to enter a new Dark Ages in which lies and magical thinking and atavistic impulses will predominate, rendering our societies dead and barren.

Lest anyone think this is an overly pessimistic view of the future, consider the baleful impact that Trump has had in a very brief amount of time. He has shown politicians and tyrants around the world that they can hold citizens in absolute contempt, feed them the most pathetically obvious untruths, and still be embraced wholeheartedly by a sufficient number of people to secure and retain political dominance. This is not a lesson that can be unlearned.

There is no way back from the Trumps and Orbans and Putins and Xis and Erdogans and Dutertes and all the other contemptible posturing halfwits who presently dominate national politics. But we know from history that when tyrants pander to the mob in order to secure power, the day is rapidly approaching when the mob takes over and burns everything down.

Our task therefore is to prepare for the time after tyranny has wrought its baleful ends. A time when, standing amid the wreckage and the rubble, a few thoughtful people will seek to rebuild in such a way as to avoid the inevitable calamities that result from failing to understand basic human limitations. Our descendants, having seen how representative democracy inevitably reduces over time to folly and ruin, will be looking for better options.

Such options need not be tainted by any present-day Political Correctness that blinds us to the reality of our situation. We have to look clearly at our situation and attempt to suggest ways to avoid ending up in the same place next time around, even though we can't foresee the circumstances of tomorrow. Just as Locke and Montesquieu and Rousseau could not have foreseen the American War of Independence that created the opportunity for some of their ideas to be adapted to emerging needs, so we cannot predict how novel ideas generated today may serve our descendants in the future. But if we fail to furnish our children and grandchildren with useful ideas from which to begin anew, we leave them merely to repeat the follies of the past and present.

Would people be happy in a society in which enfranchisement is directly connected to ability and knowledge and therefore a great many people remain unenfranchised? But is this the right question? Are people happy today? Do we have equitable societies in which each person can make best use of their abilities and feel fulfilled? Do we have societies in which equality of opportunity truly exists regardless of whether or not one is a member of "the lucky sperm club?" Even allowing for the Nordic countries where such egalitarianism is more nearly found, we can clearly answer in the negative. So there's no point in arguing for a continuation of present conditions.

It's striking that personal happiness is highest in countries that are most egalitarian and lowest in societies where wealth and opportunity are concentrated in the hands of a fortunate few. It would seem, therefore, that for people free of our current prejudices about the *status quo* a more egalitarian society based around demonstrated competence rather than hereditary caste or access to old boys' networks or other advantages based purely on accident of birth would indeed be a happier society. It would certainly be more efficient and far less prone to self-harm.

Furthermore, in a society that has no need of professional politicians and where policy is determined by qualified citizens anonymously, there is no opportunity for the kind of association between person and policy that too frequently mars contemporary politics. And finally, if policy is subject to explicit empirical review so outcomes can be assessed and defects made plain in order to be rectified, there will be little ambiguity about whether or not a policy is effective and fair. Today the vast majority of political discourse is based on assertion and presumption and increasingly on outright lies; hardly any facts are cited and those that are cited are frequently inaccurate. No political Party anywhere in the world has consistently sponsored pre-implementation modeling and post-implementation analysis to determine whether or not the policy does what it is supposed to do.

Once we get rid of elected politicians and once we enfranchise based purely on capability we dramatically diminish the probability of policy being constructed purely to win votes. And once we introduce rigorous pre-implementation analysis and post-implementation review and modification we can further reduce the prospects of inept policies causing national harm.

As for the psychological legitimacy of such a system, we know that the vast majority of us accept whatever situation we're placed in. We've accepted tribal chiefs, Barons, Emperors, Kings, Sultans and Tsars for millennia despite the fact these rulers were more often than not inept and their rules created unnecessary social havoc. In living memory we've embraced dictators and psychopaths, halfwits and incompetents. Today people all over the world feel reverence for their "strong" leaders. We are, in short, a simple-minded species.

It's difficult to believe that in future we'll feel uncomfortable with a social system that is demonstrably more fair and more efficient and entirely open to all based on individual merit rather than on ancestry or the vagaries of inherited or acquired wealth or race or religious affiliation.

Although there's no way to get to a better future until after we've passed through decades of tyrannical horror, it's plausible to imagine people accepting a far better system than representative democracy once it is instituted, provided that it does indeed address the urgent problems of society better than has been the case up until now. Although we can't get there from here, we may be able to get there after the "here" has been destroyed by the follies of populism and resulting tyranny.

A useful analogy is with evolutionary history. For the most part, evolution proceeds in a series of tiny steps as creatures adapt ever more precisely to their environments. Occasionally, however, a catastrophic event occurs that lays waste to entire ecosystems and opens up entirely new possibilities. The dinosaurs dominated our planet for hundreds of millions of years and would have continued to evolve had not a giant meteor struck the Earth and caused a mass extinction that made it possible, afterward, for mammals to emerge as the new dominant class and occupy new wide-open ecological niches.

Our political systems are subject to similar constraints: tiny alterations for as long as the old can cling on, followed by the cataclysms of tyranny that lay waste to previous certainties and permit new approaches to be attempted as the survivors stand amid the rubble and consider how best to rebuild.

Conclusion

It is easy to demonstrate that representative democracy is fatally flawed. It's based on securing a majority of votes which in turn means appealing to a majority of uninformed and relatively thoughtless citizens by means of simplistic and unrealistic promises. In order to pay for policies that buy votes, ever-increasing national debt is assumed which will burden those not yet born. The intelligent are disenfranchised because their votes are too "costly" for politicians to bother with. Costs are pushed onto those who cannot protect themselves while benefits are accrued by the unscrupulous. Short-termism pervades every decision. So representative democracy with a universal franchise is unfit for the purpose of adequate governance, the aim of which should be to secure the best possible outcome for the largest number of people in society while avoiding favoring any particular group, clique, or cabal.

In this book we've attempted to sketch a way forward that captures the gains of our present instantiations of democracy while avoiding its many systemic weaknesses. We've rejected fantasy-world solutions but instead we've used what we presently know about our hardwired primate behaviors and consequently our fundamental social and individual constraints. We've attempted to consider how we might achieve more equitable and effective governance if we were to begin from the ground up utilizing the knowledge we have gained over the last few thousand years of haphazard and largely unconscious experimentation.

This book is merely the beginning of a long process of consideration, experimentation, and continuous improvement; it is very far indeed from providing the last word on the subject.

The reader may feel there is one significant puzzle-piece missing: if such ideas are indeed better than our current implementations of self-governance, how may they be achieved? If it is true that we are about to pass into a time of darkness, how may our descendants bring back the light? This book offers no roadmap for that difficult and fraught process.

The omission is intentional for two main reasons. The first reason is that if writers on constitutional change withheld their thoughts until they could see a clear path to implementation, most would remain silent forever. Had this stricture been applied to Locke and his contemporaries, for example, the brave founders of the United States of America would have had very little to draw upon when they were considering how to structure the governance of their new nation. Earlier political and social philosophers could not possibly have foreseen the events that created the possibility whereby some of their ideas found instantiation. What mattered was that Montesquieu *et al* wrote and published and thereby pushed out into the world ideas that would be of importance to people not yet born.

The second reason there can be no road map is that there are simply too many variables to consider. It is difficult enough to predict global affairs a week hence, never mind five or ten decades ahead. Who in 1985 would have predicted the collapse of the USSR before another decade had passed and who in 1993 would have predicted that Russia would, despite all the evident horrors and misery and abject failings under communist dictatorship, fall once again under the heel of a revived dictatorship less than two decades after its nominal embrace of representative democracy and market-oriented capitalism?

Who would have predicted that the European Union, so successful in binding together nations that formerly were at war with one another every few decades, should face collapse before it reached its own seven-decade anniversary? And who, even in the midst of the calamitous George W Bush administration, would have thought that a scant eight years later the official nominee of the Republican Party would be an infantile halfwit so clearly unfit for even the most trivial form of public office that his very existence now constitutes a major threat to the entire world.

These few examples alone are enough to demonstrate that it is not possible to chart a course to the future with any confidence.

Today we can see only obstacles to any attempt to improve our systems of governance. The wealthy and powerful are content because they are at the top of the structure and can reap all its benefits while paying none of its many costs. The coterie of professional politicians have dedicated their lives to mastering the present system and any disturbance would render less valuable the time and effort they have expended over many years. Special interest groups likewise have mastered how to manipulate the present system to their advantage. And finally voters in general lack both understanding and interest in political structures. We the people are content to mouth sound-bites and repeat memes, imagining that they are our "opinions" and should be taken seriously.

Nor is there any practical way for us to effect meaningful change even if we were *en mass* supportive of a single coherent new approach. In reality of course we won't group behind a single coherent cause; rather we are divided among ourselves in terms of ideas, loyalties, interests, capabilities, and concepts. There is no "will of the people" but instead millions of different, inconsistent, and very often incoherent, "wills."

The history of the last two hundred and fifty years indicates that even when a large number of us do congregate behind a single cause, we are easily manipulated and led into disaster by charismatic charlatans. This is why we are doomed to pass through a period of tyrannies and cabals: crises resulting from democratic incapacity creates the conditions whereby the unscrupulous can claw their way to power. And history teaches one thing very clearly: those who take power in this way are always, without exception, incompetent to wield it. The final destination is always disaster.

Though the follies of populism mean the dying embers of democracy shall cast a bathetic glow, we must acknowledge that the destruction of all we value will create new opportunities. Just as the giant asteroid that slammed into the Earth sixty-five million years ago and swept away the dinosaurs made it possible for new ecosystems to emerge from the wreckage, so too will populism sweep away our verities and make it possible for new approaches to governance to come into existence.

It is only in the ruins of our dreams that we are forced, temporarily awake, to confront reality and attempt to make better accommodations with it. This book is written in the hope that at such a time in the future some of the concepts here may be of help to those who must labor to construct better alternatives to those we accept without thought today. For our descendants must eventually engage with this most important of all questions:

How may we seek to govern ourselves adequately so as to promote satisfactory outcomes for the greatest number of our people and for the precious world that we temporarily occupy?

www.ingramcontent.com/pod-product-compliance
Lightning Source LLC
Chambersburg PA
CBHW072101280526
45788CB00006B/2352